WITH OUR EYES WIDE OPEN

POEMS OF THE
NEW AMERICAN CENTURY

WITH OUR EYES WIDE OPEN

POEMS OF THE NEW AMERICAN CENTURY

EDITED BY DOUGLAS VALENTINE

WEST END PRESS

ALBUQUERQUE, NEW MEXICO
2014

Printed in the United States of America.

First Printing: April 2014

ISBN: 978-0-9910742-0-4

Typography and design by Bryce Milligan.

Contributing Editor: Julie Parson Nesbitt.

Cover art: "Nostalgia" by René H. Arceo,
colored pencil on paper, 1993.

Author photo: Michael S. Gordon, *The Republican,* Springfield, Mass.

West End Press
P.O. Box 27334
Albuquerque, NM 87125

For book information, see our web site at www.westendpress.org
West End Press • PO Box 27334 • Albuquerque, NM 87125

To Joan Joffe Hall

Contents

Part 3: Jumping Jack

Part 4: Cell Phones Burning

Appendix:

Editor's Note

"Editor" is something of an honorary title. This anthology has always been a collaborative effort among many people, especially its poets. It is an honor to have worked with them.

My original idea was to gather together a collection of poems about America's values and impact on the world. I wanted to hear what poets in other nations thought about America, its relentless wars, and its self-proclaimed "exceptionalism." I was looking, in particular, for poems about the war on terror and America's wars on Iraq and Afghanistan.

I contacted a few poet friends and they immediately understood. This initial group contributed poems and referred me to poets they admired, as well as to publishers at small political presses, activists, and organizers of poetry groups. I soon found I had a core group of advisors whose interest in the project began to shape it in unforeseen ways, as did the poems that were submitted. I learned to appreciate the central role translators play in bringing knowledge to the world.

As more poets submitted poems, the concept expanded to include the plight of exiles, immigrants, outcasts, the poor, the homeless, the working classes, and victims of race and gender discrimination. Other major themes include language, memory, and environmental degradation. Some poems encompass many themes and cannot be categorized.

Certain poems fell into place naturally. Some anchored the anthology, some gave it sparkle, and others filled in gaps in tone or style or subject matter. I began to see that the poems taken together told a story not only about America's values and impact on the world, but about the people of the world and their common humanity.

The story these poems tell is not one people will often find in conventional newspapers, magazines, or history books. Our governments will never admit that the wars they start never end—

that today, for example, children in Vietnam are still defusing unexploded American bombs. Unlike the poets in this anthology, the people who profit from war will never acknowledge the devastating effects of depleted uranium on young girls in Afghanistan, or of white phosphorus on young boys in Fallujah, or how Agent Orange affects the children of American soldiers.

There is blood, anger, fear, and sorrow in this anthology. There are ghosts of the victims of torture and death squads. There are people whose languages and customs were stolen by bankers in New York City. There are poems that will shake you from your dreams and open your eyes.

There is also hope, humor, beauty, warmth, gratitude, celebration, and transcendence. These poems tell what it means to be human. They tell how people everywhere share the same aspirations, and how people everywhere struggle for peace and justice.

It is impossible for me to say what the story ultimately means. It isn't necessary to try, of course, as the poems speak for themselves. I do believe they will help people understand the modern world.

I'd like to take this opportunity to thank John Crawford and Julie Parson Nesbitt at West End Press. I'd also like to thank Ramzy Baroud, Andy Croft, Walter Gonzalez, Kaye Hall, Jack Hirschman, Andrea Khalil, Patrice McSherry, Alison Meyers, Michael Rothenberg, Harris Schiff and Jade Zogby for their assistance. Special thanks to Eduardo Galeano for allowing West End Press to include his classic work of poetic prose, "The Nobodies," in this context.

Douglas Valentine
Longmeadow MA

PART 1:

ALABANZA

Alabanza: In Praise of Local 100

*For the 43 members of Hotel Employees and Restaurant Employees
Local 100, working at the Windows on the World restaurant,
who lost their lives in the attack on the World Trade Center.*

Martín Espada

Alabanza. Praise the cook with the shaven head
and a tattoo on his shoulder that said *Oye,*
a blue-eyed Puerto Rican with people from Fajardo,
the harbor of pirates centuries ago.
Praise the lighthouse in Fajardo, candle
glimmering white to worship the dark saint of the sea.
Alabanza. Praise the cook's yellow Pirates cap
worn in the name of Roberto Clemente, his plane
that flamed into the ocean loaded with cans for Nicaragua,
for all the mouths chewing the ash of earthquakes.
Alabanza. Praise the kitchen radio, dial clicked
even before the dial on the oven, so that music and Spanish
rose before bread. Praise the bread. *Alabanza.*

Praise Manhattan from a hundred and seven flights up,
like Atlantis glimpsed through the windows of an ancient aquarium.
Praise the great windows where immigrants from the kitchen
could squint and almost see their world, hear the chant of nations:
*Ecuador, México, República Dominicana,
Haiti, Yemen, Ghana, Bangladesh.*
Alabanza. Praise the kitchen in the morning,
where the gas burned blue on every stove
and exhaust fans fired their diminutive propellers,
hands cracked eggs with quick thumbs
or sliced open cartons to build an altar of cans.

Alabanza. Praise the busboy's music, the *chime-chime*
of his dishes and silverware in the tub.
Alabanza. Praise the dish-dog, the dishwasher
who worked that morning because another dishwasher
could not stop coughing, or because he needed overtime
to pile the sacks of rice and beans for a family
floating away on some Caribbean island plagued by frogs.
Alabanza. Praise the waitress who heard the radio in the kitchen
and sang to herself about a man gone. *Alabanza.*

After the thunder wilder than thunder,
after the shudder deep in the glass of the great windows,
after the radio stopped singing like a tree full of terrified frogs,
after night burst the dam of day and flooded the kitchen,
for a time the stoves glowed in darkness like the lighthouse in Fajardo,
like a cook's soul. Soul I say, even if the dead cannot tell us
about the bristles of God's beard because God has no face,
soul I say, to name the smoke-beings flung in constellations
across the night sky of this city and cities to come.
Alabanza I say, even if God has no face.
Alabanza. When the war began, from Manhattan to Kabul
two constellations of smoke rose and drifted to each other,
mingling in icy air, and one said with an Afghan tongue:
Teach me to dance. We have no music here.
And the other said with a Spanish tongue:
I will teach you. Music is all we have.

The Nobodies

Eduardo Galeano

Fleas dream of buying themselves a dog, and nobodies dream of escaping poverty: that one magical day good luck will suddenly rain down on them—will rain down in buckets. But good luck doesn't rain down yesterday, today, tomorrow, or ever. Good luck doesn't even fall in a fine drizzle, no matter how hard the nobodies summon it, even if their left hand is tickling, or if they begin the new day with their right foot, or start the new year with a change of brooms.

The nobodies: nobody's children, owners of nothing. The nobodies: the no ones, the nobodied, running like rabbits, dying through life, screwed every which way.

Who are not, but could be.

Who don't speak languages, but dialects.

Who don't have religions, but superstitions.

Who don't create art, but handicrafts.

Who don't have culture, but folklore.

Who are not human beings, but human resources.

Who do not have faces, but arms.

Who do not have names, but numbers.

Who do not appear in the history of the world, but in the police blotter of the local paper.

The nobodies, who are not worth the bullet that kills them.

Translated by Cedric Belfrage

Salvadoran Woman Killed on Fillmore Street

Daisy Zamora

She ran as fast as she could, she
shouted into the void, *Oh God*—
she worked so hard that day—
tightly held her purse against
her breast, then fell
in a pool of blood.

Afterwards, the kids told the police:
We didn't want to stab her we were just
desperate we only wanted her money
but she screamed so hard
she scared the hell out, she really
scared the hell out of us.

Her children were devastated, their
only support she worked double shifts
that day had forty bucks in her purse
they were waiting for her on the way
to the grocery store it was New Year's Eve,
end of the Millennium.

The newspaper also published the menu
of the dinner
                    the Mayor of San Francisco
                    was giving that night.

Of the many delicacies listed
                    was
                    wild salmon fillets
                    sprinkled with genuine gold
                                        dust.

Moulters

Rethalibe Masilo

All the while it has worked against us
in its choice of the simplest things, it
has weighed against us its darkness,
which rends the heart of a refugee,
but with which in numbers we must live,
close to millions for the dark-skinned
like me, millions of dispatched heads
who walk like shadows in the street.
When night brings a day of celebration,
like a snake losing skin we come
into a light and live in it again, the smell
of restaurants near the African quarter—
we drench ourselves with the music
of our sound, until we have to pull
back inside again. We always have to,
there are limits on liberty unexpressed
by any law document. On the train
you'll see us, carrying the continent
on our shoulders, painted bright,
though visibly concerned about papers
a back pocket is supposed to contain.
At nighttime we are spent, but bright
in the morning. Much as the train
clatters underneath to wake Paris up,
we're stopped and we're frisked again
and again, every street a new frontier.

American Sonnet (10)

Wanda Coleman

our mothers wrung hell and hardtack from row
      and boll. fenced others'
gardens with bones of lovers. embarking
      from Africa in chains
reluctant pilgrims stolen by Jehovah's light
      planted here the bitter
seed of blight and here eternal torches mark
      the shame of Moloch's mansions
built in slavery's name. our hungered eyes
      do see/refuse the dark
illuminate the blood-soaked steps of each
      historic gain. a yearning
yearning to avenge the raping of the womb
      from which we spring

Sometimes She Dreams

Laura Tohe

This woman
I call my mother
quit school in her teens to follow
                    her Grand Canyon dreams
                    where she dreams of becoming
more than maid, waitress, cook, wife.

As the bus races down the smooth highway
the magazine falls open on her lap and she fills
in her name on the white card to the
          "LaSalle Extension School of Law—
                    Learn law at home in your spare time."
But she never sends it.

Through the shiny reflection of the glass window
she sees the wooden billboards along Highway 66 near Lupton,
"See Real Indians Inside Making Jewelry, Weaving Rugs."

This isn't what her mother wanted
but she seems destined to follow the same highway
her mother took to a kitchen in California
where the dishes rattled in their cupboards.
The bus stops in front of the big hotel
where she later stripped the tightened bed covers
after the tourists left.
And outside the Canyon stretched wide her arms
                    the way her dreams must have felt
                    back then,
                    wide and open,
                              so much space to be filled.

For I Come — Death in Custody

For Brother D.L.

Lionel G. Fogarty

I
in a jail.
Even a Murri wouldn't know
if him free.
The land is not free.
Dreamtime is not free.
No money needed.
See that scarred hand at work
that's cutting away
to freedom
Freedom.
Jail not for me
but a lot of my people in jail
White jail are cruel
Set up the family, stay away
come to see your Murri
look big and grown
in learning, of our gods teaching.
What they give you in here?
Away from the corroboree
In the fuckin' jails
Murri get out, so we can fight
like the red man has done
Lord them a come.
My brother die there
in white custody
And I hate the way the screws patch up
and cover up.

He died at the white hands
it was there, in the stinkin' jails
up you might blacks
Him not free
For when white man came
it's been like a jail
with a wife and a family
black man can stay in jail
like it's home.
Fuck, they hung us all.

Beginnings of Disease

Lesego Rampolokeng

the well i spring out of that gave me a kind of birth contin-
ues to swell well into my deathyears. it was not hate so much
as a fate unwritten in king james bibles or studies of academic
analysis that struck existence disease rife. the world spun on
axis of conscience's paralysis. love was an expression of violence.
not arm-twists to get the kisses it went beyond. jaws had to be
fixed joints re-wired afterwards. mired in a circle of gravity ever
pulled downwards. a society of social retards all went channeled
towards the back of progress' bus. the back was the vantage point
to view the world. child of the street, that's where you meet
dead meat. buttocks nailed, ripped & torn through. out in the
decadence fields not of roses or wine but broken spines now
and then a kick to the chin for inspiration. kill just to get a bit
of flesh between the fingers. & then the taste never lingers. &
a life was gone in a whiff of slpiff. there's nothing to rejoice in
the issue wasn't even choice, a strike of pose a retention of poise.
among the boys the sex-thing reeked of sickness. animals get
on heat humans get their women beat down. i hear a girl speak
with pride of a beating her boyfriend gave her & understand the
epilepsy of internalisation. the grab, bite & run of the squelchy
meat. next it was guns getting the fucks for you. the knife stress-
ing your views in vaginal ears. & the tears roll acidic. & the
belt-song. standing in line to await your turn & the queue ran
on into the dawn or she went past the 'bend-without-end'. it
continued in her consciousness' absence or she got watered or
boozed into wakefulness. & it continued amid prayers without
amen its descend until boredom struck the fleshed storm limp &
fortune would let her walk away. otherwise the beyond beckoned
when semen ran out at the end of the bout & you no longer
walked to the back of the human line to refuel, stock up until it

was pumping full. went on to take another pull of the muscle… the terminal point is when the players become slayers. the rainbow's gangrenes end became amputation of humanity. you were turned to plaster if you were reluctant to be part of that human disaster & thus i cough on the mucus-flood of memories.

War Metaphysics for a Sudanese Girl

For Aciek Arok Deng

Adrie Kusserow

I leave the camp, unable to breathe,

me Freud girl, after her interior,
she "Lost Girl," after my purse,

her face:
dark as eggplant,
her gaze:
unpinnable, untraceable,
floating, open, defying the gravity
I was told keeps pain in place.

Maybe trauma doesn't harden,
packed tight as sediment at the bottom of her psyche,
dry and cracked as the desert she crossed,
maybe memory doesn't stalk her
with its bulging eyes.

Once inside the body, does war move up or down?
Maybe the body pisses it out,
maybe it dissipates, like sweat and fog
under the heat of yet another colonial God?

In America, we say, "Tell us your story, Lost Girl
you'll feel lighter,
it's the memories you must expel,
the bumpy ones, the tortures, the rapes, the burnt huts."

So Aciek brings forth all the war she can muster,
and the doctors lay it on a table, like a stillbirth,
and pick through the sharpest details
bombs, glass, machetes
and because she wants to please them
she coughs up more and more,
dutifully emptying the sticky war
like any grateful Lost Girl in America should
when faced with a flock of white coats.

This is how it goes at the Trauma Center:
all day the hot poultice of talk therapy,
coaxing out the infection,
at night, her host family trying not to gawk,
their veins pumping neon fascination,
deep in the suburbs, her life flavoring dull muzungu lives,
spicing up supper, really,
each Lost Girl a bouillon cube of horror.

Faith

Tim Seibles

Picture a city
and the survivors: from their
windows, some scream. Others
walk the aftermath: blood
and still more blood coming
from the mouth of a girl.

This is the same movie
playing all over
the world: starring everybody
who ends up where the action
is: lights, cameras, close-ups -- *that*
used to be somebody's leg.

Let's stop talking
about *God*. Try to shut up
about heaven: some of our friends
who should be alive   are no longer alive.
Moment by moment death moves
and memory doesn't remember,

not for long: even today -- even
having said
this, even knowing that
someone is stealing
our lives -- I still
had lunch.

Tell the truth. If you can.
Does it matter   who they were,
the bodies in the rubble: could it matter

that the girl was conceived by two people
buried in each other's arms, believing
completely in the world between them?

The commanders are ready. The killers
are everywhere. Almost all of them
believe in God. But somebody should

hold a note   for the Earth,
a few words for whatever being

human   could mean
beneath the forgotten sky:

some day one night,
when the city lights go out for good,

you won't believe how many stars

Jazra Khaleed

I have no fatherland
I live within words
That are shrouded in black
And held hostage
Mustapha Khayati, can you hear me?
The seat of power is in language
Where the police patrol
No more poetry cycles!
No more poet laureates!
In my neighborhood virgin poets are sacrificed
Rappers with dust-blown eyes and baggy pants
Push rhymes on kids sniffing words
Fall and get back up again: the art of the poet
Jean Genet, can you hear me?
My words are homeless
They sleep on the benches of Kladmon Square
Covered in IKEA cartons
My words do not speak on the news
They're out hustling every night
My words are proletarian, slaves like me
They work in sweatshops night and day
I want no more dirges
I want no more verbs belonging to the noncombat
I need a new language, not pimping
I'm waiting for a revolution to invent me
Hungering for the language of class war
A language that has tasted insurgency
I shall create it!
Ah, what arrogance!

Okay, I'll be off
But take a look: in my face the dawn of a new poet is breaking
No word will be left behind, held hostage
I'm seeking a new passage

Translation by Peter Constantine

At War

Metin Cengiz

At first war entered into our life by words
As if coming at us from the countryside
Even birds were carrying bullets for soldiers
We didn't know that it came on godly feet
Jumping from city to city
Entering into the games poor children played
Desperate people ate it with their bread
The government spread it like honey on our bread
Soldiers thundered and flashed lightning on streets
Lovers cut short their making love
But I took shelter in love-making day by day
Then it entered our songs with its terror
Strangling us when we breathed
It was far from our homes, but within us
For days we made it a side dish by our arrack
It was like drinking raki without water, but it happened
And some of us became heroes when we drank too much
And ceased fire, for a moment, on the battlefront
Bread was twenty times more expensive
Our lovers changed their men madly
Our parents died while waiting for peace
We became parents while waiting for peace
We could not understand why the war did not end
Then we came to know with our tiny minds
That the tumor grows within us
And dear reader, this tumor is for you.

Translated by Müesser Yeniay

State Terrorism

Dinos Siotis

I have taken to watching
the "enemies of the people"
become tattoos on the body of the state

I have taken to seeing
arrests by policemen
acting on rumors by the Party

I have taken to noticing
young men and women being shot
for unknown reasons

I met non-Party members taken to asylums
because they kept hearing machine guns

I have taken to not knowing
if I am coming or going

The Boy Who Would Die

for Motlatsi Masilo

Rethailbe Masilo

The bedroom was a shallow grave.
Perhaps the opinion of the men who came,
or of the wardrobe in that room in which a woman hid.
In any case, there was a burial in that room.
Decked in bright pajamas he slept
as bullets hunted his body,
entered the linoleum under the bed.
Men he did not know
in a house on a hill like a staircase—
from the grave you climbed to the sitting room
whose Cyclops window looked at the world,
the reason perhaps for such an act for which there was no wake,
then further up to the tin-stove kitchen
that stood above the rest, in which in winter
we sang around a pot on the stove—
if not for the outhouse some metres into the hill
the kitchen was the highest place of the house,
the closest thing to heaven we had.
No dog dared bark that night.
We lived on that hill and it lived in us, in rocks
carved out of boulders and chiseled
into bricks by able hands of noble men.
He died at the edge of his dream, a potted plant
on a winter sill, aged three, died for us;
and from then on all poems would end thus.

For Stompie

Makhosazana Xaba

Out there in freezing Moscow, news of your death brought me
    back home.
I was not a mother then but I embraced you as my son
At fourteen you were a child, so I stepped into your mother's shoes
I imagined masses in shock, joined them, questions darting in
    my head.

Out there in freezing Moscow, I took a train to the office of the
    Chief Representative
To hear his views on the news of your murder and the implicated
    Mother of the Nation
The dazzling murals at the underground stations of the city flashed,
    adding to my confusion
and my uncontainable pain about how our lives were turning into
    a national tragedy.

Out there in freezing Moscow, my elbows on my knees and my
    hands covering my face
I sat in that train and wept freezing tears for you Stompie.
    Today I am thinking:
There is a mother-to-mother feet washing exercise that needs
    to be staged, in public
for the nation to know that no fourteen year old deserves to die
    like that, not then & not now.

if he didn't keep appearing

Sarah Menefee

I walked out with a blank mind: looking at the world
on Market St where I work: there he was
legless on a wheeled board
pushing himself along
the pavement with his beautiful hands

I'd change my obsessions
if he didn't keep appearing
if they didn't keep on
reinventing him
those so sure of the rightness of their power

and the truth of us is down in Abu Ghraib
naked with upraised arms
shit spackling his back

the only supplication worth the ear of the god
of human form: the son of man

and he's not the one defiled
but those theorists of hate
with their crippled minds

Now do not tell me of men!

Müesser Yeniay

My soul hurts so much that
I awaken stones under the earth

my womanhood
a moneybox filled with stones
a home to worms, woodpeckers
a cave to the wolves climbing down my body
on my arms, new seeds are sprinkled
searching for the man of your life
is quite a serious matter

my womanhood, my cold snack
and my pubis, a home for nothingness,
the world stands here
and you! live with the rubbish thrown into you

when he is gone, tell him that torn fingernails leave flesh
that you live with the science of separation
tell him of that serious condition

like a lamb skin, I am cold in your gaze
But I am not in debt to your mother's womb, sir!
my womanhood, my invaded continent

neither am I a cultivated land...
scratch off the organ that is not mine
like a snake skin, I wish I could drop it

it is not reasonable to be mother to such a murder
it is not homeland that is divided

but the body of woman
now, do not tell me of men!

Sign of the Times

Ewa Sonnenberg

Unemployed muses on the dole have stopped believing
the words of poets. They've descended from their balconies to
    the street,
where they sell themselves in order to live. Their stomachs, not
    their wings,
dictate their choices: chastity and starving to death
or a pack of chips. They've cast off their white veils and bared
their navels. This source of their inspiration, now public property,
incites collective hymns.

Translation by Karen Kovacik

4:02 p.m.

Suheir Hammad

poem supposed to be about
one minute and the lives of three women in it
writing it and up
the block a woman killed
by her husband

poem now about one minute
and the lives of four women
in it

haitian mother
she walks through
town carrying her son's
head—banging it against
her thigh calling out
creole come see, see what
they've done to my flesh
holds on to him grip tight
through hair wool
his head all that's
left of her

in tunisia
she folds pay up into stocking
washes his european semen
off her head
hands her heart to god
and this month's rent to mother

sings berber the gold
haired one favored me, rode
and ripped my flesh, i now
have food to eat

brooklyn lover
stumbles—streets ragged under sneakers
she carries her heart
banged up against
thighs crying ghetto
look, look what's been done with
my flesh, my trust, humanity,
somebody tell me
something good

Ruins

Eliza Griswold

A spring day oozes through Trastevere.
A nun in turquoise sneakers contemplates the stairs.
Ragazzi everywhere, the pus in their pimples
pushing up like paperwhites in the midday sun.

Every hard bulb stirs.

The fossilized egg in my chest
cracks open against my will.

I was so proud not to feel my heart.
Waking means being angry.

The dead man on the Congo road
was missing an ear,
which had either been eaten
or someone was wearing it
around his neck.

The dead man looked like this. No, that.

Here's a flock of tourists
in matching canvas hats.
This year will take from me
the hardened person
who I longed to be.
I am healing by mistake.
Rome is also built on ruins.

PART 2:

LOVE AT A DISTANCE

Love at a distance:
a cycle for America

Phillippa Yaa de Villiers

I. Katrina

A cyclone is decapitating the houses
the air is full of flailing roofs, the streets are waterlogged
and politicians are at loggerheads: figureheads on a ship
that's run aground zero. Here lies the soul of our distant
civilization, replaying insanity day by daytime reruns of
the drama of despair, the theatre of confusion,
while we try to find the centre, turn our good ear
to the ground to hear the whole truth
unburdened by fear. Embedded storytellers
have kept us dumb and innocent
and the centre is nowhere near,
it is buried
deep in the heart of each of us,
wherever that is, and even though I know that
I can't understand why
I burnt another dinner tonight:
such a simple thing to get right.

II. Response Ability

A mandate is a line of dead summers in the
graveyard of the nation's memory. All that green.
Saplings chopped down by an axe-wielding icon,
a cut-out dictator with double-barreled eyes.

From Vietnam to Afghanistan and all the wars between, lies
that were told are retold; and those raised on grits and those
who sell grit bit down on the nothing that they inherited, and then
the impossible happened; hope took a look in the mirror
before stepping out on the balcony and singing a love song
to a beaten, exhausted world. No matter where you come from
a silenced heart is only one thing: dead. And when we heard his voice
we woke up in his smile and with both hands
gave him power.

III. Holding

The squeal of tyres receding into the
morning is now a memory, or a mirage:
each time she moves towards it, it dissolves.
The cross country road movie beauty pageant carnival
of politics left some time ago, and now one girl
sits tidily beside a giant cactus, the giant sun
just another father: distant and a little too warm.
It is very quiet. Her heart throbs simply like breath;
he was almost here. Almost.
His brown hands close, a father she could touch.
She wonders how it would be if he held her.
She in her little cage of fear, wild small
animal unable to trust, and he reaches for her and she
bares her teeth and snaps at him, watches him withdraw
his hurt fingers. She licks his blood from her teeth.
He'd better not disappoint. She hopes he will try again.
He won't be like all the others. But hope tastes like dust these days,
she thinks as she reaches for her last cup of water, as tanks
roll across other deserts, and buried
people cry for their lives.

A Whistle Over Belgrade

Bratislav Milanović

What kind of whistle do I hear coming from above

that is not a hawk over the flat land
that does not announce that the hunt has begun—
nor the call of the blackbird in which my heart has been hiding
when I whistled with it, once, in childhood . . .

It's not a call to wander off
into the regions where no one had been since
the time words have been written on clay, on hide or on paper,
and to recognize a new light, another shape, a dream . . .

This whistle clearly separates air
with its slash, disappears behind bricks,
into the walls where bugs have made empires
and it destroys borders between two red, hot cauldrons:

this one here and the other—on the bottom of the inconceivable.

That someone invisible, but cordial, is sending
a whistle of a bomb ready to do me a favor:
to get rid of my trivial memories,
stupid fascinations, and to liberate me of my

ruler—and just like that, on the way—of life.

Translation by Biljana D. Obradović

Crossing the Vtalva River

Lance Henson

Crossing the Vtalva River
I think of Little Wolf
In the confused distances of America
Casting a prayer so pure

Who chose the ancient belief that the
Sanctity of words
Was better than killing

So many gentle and beautiful people
For whom the stars no longer shine
The moon beyond their silence touching their
Closed eyes

Crossing the Vtalva River
I remember sweet medicine words inside
This wind

Hi niswas vita ki ni
We shall live again........

Resigned to my karma

Phomolo Lebotsa

I have a sense of purpose.
I know that what I do
Contributes to a greater whole.
It makes a difference for mankind.

I am able to rise above
Petty differences that could
Get in my way, obscure my view,
Preclude me from seeing the big picture.

I have carved a cavern for myself,
Where I crawl in, knuckle down
And get on with what it is I am good at.

I don't worry about the price of oil,
Or the anguish borne by my forefathers
As they did their bit to build a legacy
For the masters' children. All I can do
Is to know and to remember.
It is really not cold in this shell.
These fans, billowing to keep
The textiles dry, are merely contraptions
To entertain my rheumy eyes.

This is not a hard concrete floor
Numbing my feet with its iciness;
It is valuable storage space
For these finished garments
Which will soon adorn
The bodies of my brothers and sisters.

A pair of Levi's or a Gap sweater
Are commensurate to my health.
They are well worth the pain
I have started feeling in my chest these days.

I have a sense of purpose.
I know that what I do
Contributes to a greater whole.
It must be of value to the world.
How can it not be, when I get paid
Less than a dollar a day
For my pain?

American Income

Afaa M. Weaver

The survey says all groups can make more money
if they lose weight except black men ... men of other colors
and women of all colors have more gold, but black men
are the summary of weight, a lead thick thing on the scales,
meters spinning until they ring off the end of the numbering
of accumulation, how things grow heavy, fish on the
ends of lines that become whales, then prehistoric sea life
beyond all memories, the billion days of human hands
working, doing all the labor one can imagine, hands
now the population of cactus leaves on a papyrus moon
waiting for the fire, the notes from all their singing gone
up into the salt breath of tears of children that dry, rise
up to be the crystalline canopy of promises, the infinite
gone fishing days with the apologies for not being able to love
anymore, gone down inside Earth somewhere where
women make no demands, have fewer dreams of forever
these feet that marched and ran and got cut off, these hearts
torn out of chests by nameless thieves, this thrashing
until the chaff is gone out and black men know the gold
of being the dead center of things, where pain is the gateway
to Jerusalems, Boddhi trees, places for meditation and howling
keeping the weeping heads of gods in their eyes.

Sharon

Aharon Shabtai

Why do they love Sharon? Because he is heavy he is wide he
is stuffed, has invisible edges, but he is whole, continuous, and
he rises, and rises again, always rolling. And when he sits it all
comes to him, meat, money, real estate. For he is not weak, not
transparent, doesn't tremble as a leaf, but is sealed, viscid, with
thickness, not crispy, he is flexible, usable, lies around, crouches,
takes over space, shelters, hides, fences, blocks. For he opens his
mouth, gluttonous, swallows, unashamed to take a meat ball off
the table with the cartons of fries, teaches to satisfy the appetite,
to take things, to enlarge the mass, the territory, the quantities.
For he opens cracks, windows, roads in the landscape, breaks
even through cement or iron, but always closes it as well, cuts
off corners, remembers to lock up, to fortify, doesn't leave a crack
for a lizard, but reaches his arm as if through a sleeve of doubt,
and seals it all, with a wall, with a tank, with housing, with own-
ership, with a platoon. For he smiles, smiles as a round man,
rounds things up, moves around like a pancake, bypasses, flanks,
circles, and returns again in a different cycle. For he shares his
smile generously, and everyone is invited to smile, even in the
mud, even over the pool of blood. For he sticks his hand in the
pocket, elbows, pats on the back. For he commands, moves peo-
ple, moves vehicles, moves houses, moves a tree, a field, borders.
For he carries the wars in his arms like suitcases, as if heading
for a trip. And everything within them is organized, the living
and the dead, like folded shirts, ironed underwear, clean socks,
handkerchiefs. Suitcase by suitcase all lined up, each made of
shiny leather, with a padded leather handle, accessorized at the
corners, with shiny nickel buckles and bolts. For if he will go,
disappear, he will no longer be heavy, wide, stuffed, with invis-
ible edges. He will be incomplete, incontinuous, won't rise and

rise again, will never roll. He will not sit, and nothing will come to him. Not meat, not money, not real estate. For he will be weak, transparent, will tremble as a leaf, will be unsealed, inviscid, not thick, crispy, inflexible, unusable, will never lie around, won't crouch, won't take over space, will not shelter, not hide, not fence, not block. For he won't open his mouth, won't be gluttonous, won't swallow, won't take a meat ball off the table with the cartons of fries. He won't teach: not to satisfy the appetite, not to take things, and not to enlarge the mass, the territory, the quantities. He won't open cracks, windows, roads in the landscape, won't even break through cement or iron, and will never close anything, won't cut off corners, won't remember to lock up, to fortify, he will leave a crack for a lizard, won't reach his arm as if through a sleeve of doubt, and won't seal, not with a wall, not with a tank, not with housing, not with ownership, nor with a platoon. He won't smile, will never smile as a round man, won't round things up, won't move around like a pancake, bypass, flank, circle, and won't return again in a different cycle. He won't share his smile generously, and won't encourage anyone to smile, not in the mud, not over the pool of blood. He won't stick his hand in his pocket, won't elbow, won't pat on the back. He won't command, won't move people, won't move vehicles, won't move houses, won't move a tree, a field, a border. He shall not carry the wars in his arms like suitcases, as if heading for a trip, and nothing, neither the living nor the dead, will be organized like folded shirts, ironed underwear, clean socks, handkerchiefs. The suitcases will no longer stand, lined up suitcase by suitcase, each made of shiny leather, with a padded leather handle, accessorized at the corners, with shiny nickel buckles and bolts.

Unwanted Neighbors

Paul Polansky

Dimitri, a Russian-Jew who teaches
history at a university in the United States,
told me there was only one solution
to the Jewish-Palestinian problem:
transport all the Arabs away.

He didn't tell me where the Palestinians
should be taken, but a few days later
in the *Jerusalem Post*
a Jewish religious leader proposed
all Palestinians be relocated
to the Sinai desert.

In the Czech Republic, several political leaders
wanted to put Czech Gypsies on reservations
like America did with its Indians.

That's the problem with America
being the only world-power today.
Everyone looks to see how
the United States solved its
unwanted neighbor problem.

A Confession

Samah Sabawi

I stand between my shame and relief
I breathe...
The missiles missed this time
Truth is, they didn't really miss

Someone's house is destroyed
but not the house I know so well
Someone's family is grieving
but not the one whose name I carry
I linger...
between my shame and relief
I breathe...
I... breathe...
I tell myself
'this flesh, torn and scattered,
is not flesh I have ever embraced.'
I soothe myself,
'Nor are these small lifeless hands
the ones with a crayon I've traced.'
I...breathe...
This time...the missiles missed
those whose names are engraved on my lips
This time
they didn't stop
those hearts beating in my chest
They live...
I breathe...
But I must confess
Every time the bombs fall on Gaza
I search for answers

Where did they strike?
Which street did they blow up?
Which neighborhood did they destroy?
Which lives did they steal?
Aware of my guilt I whisper a prayer
Dear God, please don't let it be the ones I know.
Dear God, please don't let it be the ones I love.
Dear God....
Ya Allah...
Ya Allah...

And when it's over
And while a less fortunate family weeps
I stand between shame and relief
I breathe...
I breathe...
Thank God my loved ones were spared
This time.

Poem for Samah

Lia Tarachansky

Habibti
For a moment
We were in each other
For a moment we were intertwined,
Bombed into the same consciousness

Bomb bomb bombed
Until I was not an Israeli
Until you weren't a Palestinian
We were each other
For a moment Habibti

For a moment,
Habibti,
They were not my missiles that missed you
It was not my army that marched in, to you
It was not your grief you carried
Not your war scars or your memories

Habibti,
For a moment
Our pasts were no longer bordered
We were in each other,
Habibti
And your pain was heard

With every resonating call to prayer
My pain was heard
With every barked order

It's not an issue of forgiveness
Or rhythm or justice
There is no end or contiguity
For we are bombed into the same existence
Bombed
Until my eyes can't squeeze shut
Until the shrieking and twisting of smoky paths through the sky
Pried open your hands from your ears with fear
I listened, Habibti,

Past every rocket launcher
With a remote-controlled machine gun in my hands
I heard you,
Habibti,
For a moment
The words shot at me with every trigger pull I pulled
Your words shot at me,
Your words shot at me,
Were launched, like seeds pollinating the silent fields
Like neglected olives that fall, beating against the sacs
Someone once picked
And they exploded
More powerful
More traumatizing
Louder
Than the first explosion
Louder
Than that explosion that killed Ibrahim
Louder than the rocket that missed Murjana
By an inch

In that moment,
I take responsibility. Here.
I have no explanations
I have no beef to pick with you
Nothing.

For a moment,
You are inside me
Habibti,
I hear you.

The Shadow

Valerio Magrelli

    Sunday morning
I'm woken by my daughter's voice
who shouting
asks her brother
if it's true the Bomb
when it explodes
leaves the shadow
of man on the wall.
(Not of "a man"
but "of man" she says.) He
agrees that it does.
I turn in my bed.

Translation by Jamie McKendrick

Their Screams Live in My Ears

Pina Piccolo

Sixty years later, he said on the air:
"Then I was the foolish young soldier
Who two days after the atomic bomb
On August 8, 1945
Tried to pick up the shadow
Of the girl
Embossed
On the sidewalk."

Meekly he continued to say it
Gentle old Japanese man
No longer a soldier
So around the world
People wouldn't cover their ears
At the screams
Of two Iraqi sisters
Fifteen and sixteen
(Never knew their names
Newspapers never bothered)
Slaughtered
By soldiers
Who saw a branch move
In the woods
As the girls picked up kindling
To warm up the hearth
In the coldest December in
Fifty years

"Their screams live in my ears"
To be heard over

Top volume rock
"We are the champions"
(Master of space, soon to be
Lords of the universe)
Issuing from a depleted uranium
Shielded tank
As it blindly trumpets its way
Through the streets of Falluja.

Their screams live in my ears
Never sleep
Don't ever nestle comfortably
In the crook of my ear
An unresigned whisper
Raw, like the first day
They roar
To be heard
Angry, unforgiving
Surprised, aghast.

Your Poems Are So Political

Margaret Randall

Your poems are so political
the academy darling says,
implying deficiency
or some vague naiveté
as if I should know better at my age.

What moves me is the delicate membrane
where love's pulse
beats against submission,
subjugation erases will,
Big Guy versus everyone else.

Your gentle fingers braid mine
as we transit streets
where it's a crime
to love
outside the rules.

Shame as an acceptable place to be,
God with a capital G,
water wasted or poisoned
beneath a desert carved into greedy squares
crowding against my undulating bluffs.
Children who will never grow up,
who know there is nothing
to live for
but insist with a child's guile
they want to live.

War is never somewhere else, ravaging
a country of people I do not know
who look different
and whose words I cannot understand.
Every war ignites my fever.

Melting glaciers raise the level
of oceans
but also the bile rising from my gut.
When you know better you do better
seems to have lost its relevance.

Yes, I respond, *my poems are political
like a razor against your throat,
the word no when you expected yes,
spit in the eye of the powerful
my poems challenge every crime.*

PART 3:

JUMPING
JACK

Jumping Jack
The M16 Mines

Teresa Mei Chuc

In standing position
with arms to the side,

jump while
spreading the legs
and lift arms
above the head.

Jump back into
standing position
and up again,
spreading the legs
and lifting the arms
above the head.

Repeat

When a M16 landmine
is triggered, it will
spring into the air
and explode with
a capacity to level
everything in a
150 metre radius.

Deadly shrapnel
spreading
a further 350 metres.

Metal casings
from an unexploded
bomb can fetch
25,000 Vietnamese dong
or $1

for a poor family
in Vietnam.

Men comb
the forests
and beaches
of Quang Tri
looking for the metal
that will feed their family,
risking their lives.

Children working
in the fields think it's
a toy they've found.

Nguyen was hoeing
a small piece of land
his parents gave him
when an unexploded
U.S. military bomb
was triggered
and blew off both
his hands.

M-16A2 Assault Rifle

Hugh Martin

Some days I clean the rifle so it shines,
A cold slice of darkness in grease-stained hands.
Some days, I hate to take it outside, dust
Blowing faster, eating the morning brown.
Some days, after the warm silhouettes bow
Across the green field of the firing range,
I sit against sandbags, sweat in sunlight,
And hold that grip, the muzzle's edge resting
Across the top of my thigh. And some days,
When I've cleaned it for hours, I want only
To take it home for the space of blue wall
Above the mantel, because it'd be wrong
To shoot again, to smear and smudge with whorls,
To blemish a thing that makes the night blush.

Names of the Dead

Floyd Cheung

from *The New York Times*
November 24, 2009

CLEAVER
FRAZIER
HAND
SHERMAN

Staff Sergeant
Sergeant
Lance Corporal
Sergeant

John
Daniel
Nicholas
Benjamin

Marysville, Washington
St. Joseph, Michigan
Kansas City, Missouri
Plymouth, Massachusetts

36
25
20
21

Beloved
Beloved
Beloved
Beloved

Names of the Dead II

Floyd Cheung

of the ones we don't know
of the ones not published in *The New York Times*

of those who fight on the other side
of those who are caught in between

of their hometowns, ages, and
by whom they are beloved

The Black Camel
Malak al-Maut (Azrael), the Angel of Death
Lance Corporal Aaron Austin
Republican Guard Colonel Mohammed Hamed

Death is the Black Camel that kneels before every door.
—Arabic saying

No one has been here
before you, no one will come
after you're gone.

David Allen Sullivan

I carry your pic
inside my helmet. You're my
lucky ace of spades,

Tiffany. Come spring
I aim to be home and slip
that rock on your hand.

                    Barracks were a wreck.
          Men were looting everything:
              guns, chairs, even cots.

                    I threatened to shoot.
      One locked eyes with me and grinned,
               Why do such a thing?

Metal coffee cans
are stuffed with bolts, nails, even
Iraqi coins cut

into star-shaped chunks.
Some get detonated by
remote-controlled cars.

The mass of flies lifts,
resettles as I scoot past
the dead body's bloat.

Don't cling to one form;
water continues to flow
after the pot breaks.

Americans tore
the small *Qu'ran* from my wife's
neck, made me burn it.

Grilled the Twinkies you sent.
They laughed, but New Mexico
and you were right here.

I don't ask for much:
my teashop, some customers,
our good wives at home.

My son wanted more.
Worked for Americans, told them
what Iraqis said.

We asked a farmer,
face darkened by his raised spade,
if he'd seen any

foreign fighters. Ali,
our Iraqi terp, laughed, then
translated: *Yes, you.*

                                        Ali wore a mask,
                                   like a criminal, but the
                                   Mujahid still knew.

            Blood, frogs, lice, wild beasts.
            Murrain, boils, thunder and hail.
                Locusts and darkness.

The RPG slammed
into the Humvee's windshield
but didn't explode.

Derrick took the wheel
'cuz I got jittered, big ol'
bomb point in his face.

                The slaughter of firstborns.
            Glass, mingled with fire, will fall,
                break angels' harp strings.

Didn't feel a thing,
just a pinging in my ears.
I looked, and Derrick

and where he'd been was
just gone. Scarved men were dragging
Ali through glass shards.

                                    I made them take me
                                to where it happened. Frenzy
                                    of soldiers and swears.

The terp's old man stood
still as a deer while soldiers
humped, picking up pieces.

                              Blood filled a tire track.
                       Filmed over with dust. Dimpled
                                  in a tear of wind.

The IED hit
while I held his cigarette.
Where's God, Tiffany?

Blood dried on my lip,
but it wasn't mine. Didn't
wash it off for days.

                           The morgue's waiting room
                        monitors scrolled through faces
                            of the dead: May, June . . .

                             Swore I saw my son,
                       but when they showed me, I cried
                                for a stranger boy.

                    If it does not hurt
          nothing will grow. Pierce your tongue.
              Spot ground with blood. Pray.

Blood on the letter
ripped apart in Derrick's gear:
Dear Sis, I never . . .

                                 I still hope to find
                             his body. Bury it. Black
                              Camel kneels before

                                every door, but why
                       take our eldest so soon? Love
                                has no taste in war.

These sandals were made
only for you, but now I
place them in the fire.

Shake 'n' Bake

"Gingerbread White House: View of the North Portico,
100 pounds (34 sheets) of gingerbread;
150 pounds of white and dark chocolate;
clear, poured sugar windows;
one strand of white lights inside the
Gingerbread White House make it glow."
—White House Press Release, Christmas 2005

Tim Thorne

Make it glow. Make it glow. Make it glow.
White phosphorus over Fallujah, a hundred times sheet lightning:
the *illuminati* stagger out,
ripping away clothes, skin.
What were handfuls of flesh pour between fingers.
Breathing fluid fire, the too-bright smell,
they are not dead. Thirty seconds, forty-five,
then the high explosive follow-up
and all their Christmases come at once,
as the saying goes.

Every child knows about the witch in the gingerbread house,
about the glow from ovens.
Jenna and Barb jr are too grown-up
to play "knock-knock" at the sugar panes, to dare each other.
Fairy tales belong to the land
of faraway, of Scheherazade, saved by stories,
whose statue in Iraq has not been toppled.
Her saying goes and goes. She goes, "Onceuponatime..."
There was a city. A strand of white lights
made it glow.

Inanna Moaning

Sabah Mohsen Jasim

Grandma, you're still young!
Your braids have been released over the Tigris and Euphrates
Like twin fishes, rejoicing,
While I come out just to watch with surprise.
Those, the promised ones, used to call me 'Gypsy,'
And while they were stealing everything I had,
They tied my legs & hands
They blindfolded my eyes
And muzzled my mouth,
And now it's hard for me to act,
Grandma,
My whole body convulses,
I am helpless,
No more alive than Lamassu.
They poured volcanoes of hot water on me,
They uprooted my throat with a harsh flint stone
For fear of me shouting:
"Those American missiles
Will target your heart!"

That which is knocking,
Is not the sound of moon kisses, impressed on a lake,
Or the approaching night,
Or a worshiper's hymns.
What's left within me would listen:
(Freedom is what a man must exercise!)
While the knocker,
The thing that is coming,
The rejecting, protesting of truth throbbing,
Is but my heart.

So bless me, Grandma,
And heal my deep wounds
Those drowned deep with my insurgent tearing.
All that's left is
Their desire for the barbecue,
While my heart is still throbbing with love,
A heart I will never abandon,
That will never give up singing!

Just as I promised, I dedicate this
Song to you, Inanna.
Stop wailing now, it hurts my wound
And quickens my heart,
My heart, a promising seed:
None would know except you, Grandma,
Wherefrom it had got its glowing color,
Of Babylon sun, of red anemones
And lightning sky, together.

Rueful Outlays for a Conscript

Linh Dinh

Minus the moneyed, defective and ministers of religion,
What is left is sucked into the intake, paid some fraction
Of what they deserve, trained for a period of months,
Then spat out, in one piece or several, adding no value,
Really, no advantage to this high-tech peace machinery.

This churning that takes place requires
An enormous amount of effort in training,
And then they were gone…

No two-bit fruit-peeling racket,
No cookie monster slicer and sorter,
No depleted uranium sushi fridge,
No wine chiller with blinking canopy,
No spiral dough kneader and mixer,
No candy-assed gelato churner,
No, Sir, this is a real meat grinder.

VA Hospital Confessional

Brian Turner

Each night is different. Each night the same.
Sometimes I pull the trigger. Sometimes I don't.

When I pull the trigger, he often just stands there,
gesturing, as if saying *Aren't you ashamed?*

When I don't, he douses himself
in gasoline, drowns himself in fire.

A dog barks in the night's illuminated green landscape,
and the platoon sergeant orders me to shoot it.

Some nights I twitch and jerk in my sleep.
My lover has learned to face away.

She closes her eyes when I fuck her. I imagine
she's far away, and we don't use the word *love*.

When she sleeps, helicopters
come in low over the date palms.

Men are bound on their knees, shivering
in the animal stall, long before dawn.

I whisper into their ears, saying
Howlwin? Howlwin?—meaning—*Mortars? Mortars?*

Howl wind, motherfucker? Howl wind?
The milk cow stares with its huge brown eyes.

The milk cow wants to know
how I can do this to another human being.

I check the haystack in the corner
for a weapons cache. I check the sewage sump.

I tell no one, but sometimes late at night
I uncover rifles and bullets within me.

Other nights I drive through Baghdad.
Firebaugh. Bakersfield. Kettleman City.

Some nights I'm up in the hatch, shooting
a controlled pair into someone's radiator.

Some nights I hear a woman screaming.
Other nights I shoot the crashing car.

When the boy brings us a platter of fruit,
I mistake cantaloupe for a human skull.

Sometimes the gunman fires into the house.
Sometimes the gunman fires at me.

Every night it's different.
Every night the same.

Some nights I pull the trigger.
Some nights I burn him alive.

Iraqi Poets Society

Julia Stein

That day Abdullah al-Baghdadi watched the huge statue
of the tyrant Saddam knocked down,
falling on its back,
a rope around its neck,
he dreamed of an Iraqi Dead Poet's Society,
searched for all the lost poets in Baghdad,
sent letters, taxis and messengers across the city
looking for the hiding poets,
the suffocated poets,
the lost poets,
the banned poets,
the poets who had spent three decades
like the walking dead.

He had dreams the suffocated poets
would have air to breathe,
the hiding poets would walk the streets,
the lost poets would be found
at a new Poetry Headquarters in Baghdad,
the banned poets would now meet weekly
for readings and publish in a monthly magazine,
the poets who had been the walking dead would resurrect to
invite Westerners to come to Baghdad to read and
to meet Iraqi poets now reborn.

In the first months when the poets resurrected and
sent al-Baghdadi messages,
his dreams grew that poems would erase
all the roadside bombs,
the concrete blast barriers,

the blown up cars,
poems to rebuild his country verse by verse,
poems to erase the scars of the tyrant's torture,
stanzas to heal the broken human hearts,
verses to shore up the economy

They found a building by the Tigris.
Iraqi poets now were breathing poems again.
For a few days, a few weeks, a few months, poems sprouted and
grew like a huge bush spreading
out over their building--
a virtual forest explosion of poems marched
up and down the Baghdad streets

when they began the terrible count:
"One poet was threatened. One was kidnapped.
One was killed. One fled abroad."

Still al-Baghdadi held onto his poems, his building,
when suicide bombs exploded on the street
leaving corpses and the wounded.
The warring militias grew,
divided up the neighborhoods.
Refugees fled in cars packed with suitcases.

The poets felt policemen born in their heads,
the inner cops growing in their skulls,
barbed wire grew around their hearts.

When a car bomb blew up Baghdad's poetry HQ,
Al-Baghdadi stood still, "squinting through
the dust and debris," watching the debris
flying through the air in all directions.

The Iraqi Curator's PowerPoint

for Donny George Youkhanna, 1950–2011,
Curator of the Iraq National Museum

Philip Metres

You can see the footprints around the hole
The Iraqi Curator said. They smashed the head
Because they could not lift it from the base,
This statue of Nike. It's still missing.
And this is *Umma Al-Ghareb*, my dig site.
The Mother of Scorpions, it means. *Y'anni,*

Next slide: more damage by looters. If the eyes
Are gems, they will be made into holes.
If the skin is gold, goodbye. Now this is a sight:
The bodies are too heavy, so they took the heads
Of these terracotta lions. A slide is missing
Here. What I ask you is this: base

What you believe on what you can almost see.
For example: you hear the dogs bay
From the outskirts of the city. They head
Wherever they smell flesh. My eyes
Still see buildings that are now holes.
What you see is not what is missing.

Next slide. I'd heard that Etana, missing
For years, was in Damascus. Then in Beirut.
Then, I got a call from an art friend, a whole
Continent away. Does it have a scratch at the base
Of his hand and along the chest I said he said yes
Of course I said it is headless.

And writing on the shoulder beneath no head
And he said yes and yes the right arm missing
And I said my God I said John take my eyes
And let me see. I was blind and now had sight
Though I could not see it. This is the basis
Of art, *sadiki*. There's something beyond the hole

Which each must face. Missile sites. Army bases.
The hole in the ground where thousands climbed
Into the sky. Missing heads of state. Eyes.

Drone

...Let this be the Body
through which the War has passed.
—Frank Bidart

Solmaz Sharif

somewhere I did not learn *mow down or mop up* • somewhere I
wouldn't hear *your father must come with me* or *I must fingerprint your
grandmother can you translate please* • the FBI has my cousins' comput-
ers • my father says *say whatever you want over the phone* • my father
says *don't let them scare you that's what they want* • my mother has a
hard time believing anything's bugged • my father and I always talk
like the world listens • my father is still on the bus with contraband
papers under his seat as uniforms storm down the aisle • it was my
job to put a cross on each home with dead for clearing • it was my
job to dig graves into the soccer field • I wrote *red tracksuit* • I wrote
Shahida, headless, found beside Saad Mosque • *buried in the same grave
as the above* • I wrote *unidentified fingers* • *found inside Oldsmobile car*
• I wrote their epitaphs in chalk • from my son's wedding mattress
I know this mound's his room • I dropped to a knee and engaged
the enemy • I emptied my clip then finished the job • I took two
steps in and threw a grenade • I took no more than two steps into
a room before firing • in Haditha we cleared homes Fallujah style
• my father was reading the Koran when they shot him through
the chest • they fired into the closet • the kitchen • the 90-year-old
standing over the stove • just where was I • *uno a uno tu cara en
todos los buses urbanos* • *Here lie the mortal remains of one who in life
searched your face* • call me when you get home • let's miss an
appointment together • let's miss another flight to repeated strip
searches • that Haditha bed • magenta queen sheets and a wood-
shelved headboard and blood splattered up the walls to the
ceiling • they held each other • they slept on opposing ends

wishing one would leave • mother doesn't know who I am anymore • I write *Mustapha Mohammad Khalaf, fifteen months old* • I write *Here lies an unknown martyr, a big security guard with a blue shirt, found near an industrial area with a chain of keys* • *Martyr unknown, only bones* • they ask if I have anything to declare then limit my response to fruits and nuts • an American interrupts an A and B conversation to tell me *you don't have to do anything you don't want to do* • he strikes me as a misstep away from *she was asking for it* • what did you expect after fishing Popov from a trash bin • what did you expect after accepting a marbled palace • they drag the man who killed my uncle out of a hole • they inspect him for ticks on national television • no one in my family celebrates • when the FBI knocks I tell them *I don't have to do anything I don't want to do* they get a kick out of that • she just laid there and took it like a champ • she was dying for it • at a protest a man sells a shirt that says *My dick would pull out of Iraq* • my mother tape-records my laugh to mail bubble-wrapped back home • my mother records me singing *Ye shabe mahtab mah meeyad to khab* • I am singing the moon will come one night and take me away sidestreet by sidestreet • sitting on a pilled suburban carpet or picking blue felt off the hand-me-down couch • the displaced whatnots • I practice the work of worms • how much I can wear away with no one watching • two generations ago my blood moved through borders according to grazing and seasons • then a lifeline of planes • planes fly so close to my head filled with bomblets and disappeared men • scaffolding sprouts nooses sagging with my dead • I burn my finger on the broiler and smell trenches • my uncle pissing himself • shopping bags are legs there is half a head in the gutter • I say *Hello NSA* when I place a call • somewhere a file details my sexual habits • some tribunal may read it all back to me • Golsorkhi, I know the cell they will put me in • they put me onto a crooked pile of others to rot • is this what happens to a brain born into war • a city of broken teeth • the thuds of falling • we have learned to sing a child calm in a bomb shelter • I am singing to her still

Afghanistan

Tahar Bekri

If music were to die
If love is the work of Satan
If your body is your prison
If the whip is what you know how to wield
If your heart is your beard
If your truth is a veil
If your refrain is a bullet
If your song is a funeral prayer
If your falcon is a crow
If your look is brother to dust

How can you love the sun in your lair?

If your sky detests kites
If your soil is a minefield
If your wind is thickened by powder
And not fecund pollen
If your mulberry tree is a gallows
If your door is a barrage
If your bed is a trench
If your house is a coffin
If your river flows with blood
If your snow is a cemetery

How can you love the water in the river?

If your mountains submit
Humiliated and humbled
Their backs unjust citadels
Their guts disemboweled to harden stone

If your valley is not to fuel your dream
Like a rose in the zephyr
If your clay is kneaded by grief
Not to raise a school
Like an apricot tree in flower
If your reed is not a qalam

How can you live in the light?

If your labour is seed for scarecrows
Craven cache for poppies
If your horse is enslaved by your blinkers
Scorns the flight of flutes in the air
If your valley vomits its sapphires
To the warlords
If the braids of women are ropes
If your stadium is a slaughterhouse
If your path is invisible
If your night is a tomb for the stars

How can you promise the moon?

If Ghengis Khan is your master
If your child is the offspring of Timur
If your face is faceless
If your sabre is your executioner
If your epic is ruins and vultures
If all the rain in the world cannot wash your forefinger
If your desire is dead wood
If your fire is ash
If your flame is smoke
If your passion is grenades and cannon

How can you seduce the dove at the window?

If your village is a casern
Not a nest for swallows
If your house is a cave
If your source is a mirage
If your dress is your shroud
If death is your mausoleum
If your Koran is a turban
If your prayer is war
If your paradise is hell
If your soul is your sombre gaoler

How can you love the spring

Translation by Patrick Williamson

... Again they're off for their Afghanistan

Elena Fanailova

... Again they're off for their Afghanistan,
And black roses in Grozny, big as fists
On the plaza, as they form a square
On their way to being smashed to bits.
When they go to get sworn in,
She flies to give it up to him,
Like a new-fangled Tristan and Isolde
(Special dispatch to all posts)
And there's a strange strain of the Hep in Ashkhabad

He drinks magnesia from the common trough,
Making a racket with the metal chain
While she recites Our Father at the doctor's
Counting the days of menstrual delays.
The cure proceeds at its own pace,
And meanwhile he carouses like a boy
Bored and jerking away his days.

Corporal N., a bit older than the rest,
Is still a little wet behind the ears,
Is an expert in the vulgar furlough arts,
He pours black wine for them,
Remembering, not from the authorized
Sections, but something along these lines:
The diseases of dirty hands are
Swallowed bullets made of shit

Common myth and communal hell.
She's off to the abortion clinic,
Exactly as the doctor has prescribed,
Like a soldier marching the familiar march,

According to the commander's drill.
And there she is, surrounded by her friends,
Slender and skittish fauns and dryads all—
Cattle at an abattoir.
There's no free will,
Just chance, the luck to simply stay alive.

And there in 'Ghanistan were beer-soaked mustaches,
Fucking beautiful Uzbek girls
Unbraiding bridles with their tongues.
They got to ride on armor metal,
Fast and crude.
Later, to keep the whole affair from leaking out,
The colonel himself shot them dead
In front of the regiment—or more precisely,
Had them shot, the ones who dragged
The girls into the bushes by their braids
And those who raped them in the bushes,
The Afghan girls who looked about sixteen,
But weren't any older than twelve, and barely.
The rapists weren't more than twenty.
Their families heard nothing of it.
And the ceiling bore down slowly
Like a chopper to the sound of women wailing

Now they're at the river getting soused
And reminiscing about the good old days.
And it's as though a strange chill tugs
Against their corporeal flesh.
Now the lovers are both forty.
Or, more precisely, the husband and wife.
The kid is ten, they had him late by Soviet standards.
Their scars speak for themselves.

I'll never find another country such as this.

Translation by Genya Turovskaya and Stephanie Sandler

PART 4:

CELL PHONES
BURNING

Why Rabbits Never Sleep

Menka Shivdasani

Lettuce is Nature's sedative, I read somewhere,
so at three a.m., I finally
decided to make a little salad.
There were cockroaches in the refrigerator
but I washed the vegetable well, then peeled
layer after layer, startling a sleepy worm
that had crawled indignantly from beneath the leaves.

But the pieces lay untidily, splashed across the plate,
like splotches of sun on the street;
so I tried another strategy - common, really,
any housewife-poet will know about it.

I took a knife, its blade seductive in the dark,
and I chopped. The fragments, I noticed, as I yawned,
had begun to take the most extraordinary shapes.
Somewhere I recognised a bride,
her toenails turned to ash,
a mother-in-law and husband shut the door.
Another piece bore the face of a politician;
a third was a child with eyes wide open.
And why did the dish resemble
a wounded Hiroshima?

I went at it like the smiling Nazi
in a half-remembered film, who invited
his prisoner to lunch, then demonstrated
the art of cutting carrots.
"Chop, chop," he said, and as the slices fell,
still smiling, hacked the prisoner's finger off,

two actually, with the words, "Chop, chop,"
and another smile.

That night, I discovered the reason
rabbits never seem to sleep.

Sunday Bath

For Farooq

Rafiq Kathwari

I

My sister latched the door:
A tube of light through the pane
stunned the cement floor.

My kid brother and I sat
naked near a bucket,
a canister to scoop water

Lifebuoy soap on chipped saucer,
a cylindrical container poised on bricks,
faucet crudely soldered to hem.

Under the container,
nuggets glowed on a charcoal burner
heating up the water.

Let's be clear about this: No
shower, no tub, no sink, no mirror,
only a hole in the floor

for draining waste bath water out to a gully.
To be fair to bathrooms he had known,
Father had named it the Cube.

II

Dizzy and nauseous, heart faster,
beads of sweat on bony chest,
the more I breathed, the more I gasped,

wondering what was taking my sister
so long to scoop water from the bucket
and shower it on my head.

She dragged herself to the door
on tip-toe to reach the latch, fell back,
slowly rose, her fingers clawing the pane.

My kid brother collapsed
on the floor, his mouth an O.
Are we playing dead?

Charcoal, the Mother of All Coals,
Father later said, burns quickly
in airtight rooms, releases deadly gas.

You can't see, smell, or taste it.
Inhaled, it displaces oxygen
we breathe to stay alive.

I remember only blurs: glass
shattering, treetops waving, sirens,
a cold mask on my face: breathing.

III

Farooq, older brother, waiting
his turn to bathe, sat on a small
crate outside the Cube, reading

Superman, wondered
why no waste water flowed
out to the open gully

in the courtyard. He bolted upstairs
to tell Father, who ran down
without touching the handrail,

broke the pane, unlatched the door,
dragged us all out, and sent Farooq
on his Hero bike to summon Red Cross.

IV

My sister gradually grew
protective of me and my kid brother
who stopped sucking his thumb, after all.

Praised for his presence of mind,
Farooq promised but never gave me his comics
and never lets us forget his heroics.

V

Seeing her three angels in mortal poses,
Mother ripped her blouse,
pummeled her bosom. "There is no god

but God, no god but God, no god."
The next day, my parents sacrificed
a lamb, gave meat to refugees

camped in Murree
near the Cease Fire Line,
after the first war over Kashmir.

Tears

Dunya Mikhail

I work in a store for selling tears
in bottles of various sizes and shapes.
Crowded place, and no time
to bring handkerchiefs.
First in line is the woman
who comes every day
to buy these colorless drops.
For herself? For others?
Next, a newcomer.
He thought he would not leave his country
even if the mountain was removed from its place.
Next is a little boy with his grandmother.
They survived the flood, not exactly.
The woman at the end of the line
wants to return her bottle of tears.
She says it's not opened.
She thought she would need it
after the departure of her friend.
But she, instead,
kept going back and forth
between two parking spaces.
The sun left to the other half of the world.
Time to go home.
We are out of tears.

Passage to Exile

Adnan al-Sayegh

The moaning of the train echoes the sorrow of tunnels
as it roars along rails of dogged memories.
Half my heart's nailed to the window
while the other half
plays poker with a girl whose skirt exposes her thighs.
Painfully, she asks
why my fingers are falling apart
like the wood of spent coffins.
Quickly, as if afraid at not being able to hold on to anything,
I tell her about my Homeland:
the fluttering banners,
the colonization,
the glory of the Nation,
the sex in public bathrooms.
With her wet hair she leans over my teary face
and claims she doesn't understand.
Meanwhile, in the far corner,
Mozart scatters his notes over snow-covered valleys.
I tell her my Homeland's sad beyond reason,
that my songs are aggressive, refractory, and shy.
I tell her I'll lie down on the first sidewalk I find in Europe
and hold my feet up
so pedestrians can see the traces of school beating bastinados,
and the ones from jails—
the injured soles that drove me here.
I carry no passport in my pocket,
just a history of oppression.
For fifty years we've been subsisting on an animal diet
of pre-packaged speeches
and hand-rolled cigarettes

as we stand before the gallows
watching our own hanging corpses swing.
Too fervently we applaud the rulers,
fearful for our families
whose files fill basements of secret-service buildings.
Homeland!
begins each president's speech
and *Homeland!* ends each president's speech,
and in between there are the president's streets the president's
songs the president's museums the president's gifts the presi-
dent's trees the president's factories the president's newspapers
the president's stables the president's clouds the president's boot
camps the president's statues the president's bakeries the presi-
dent's medals the president's mistresses the president's schools
the president's farms the president's water the president's orders
the president's . . .

She will stare for a long time
at my rain-and-spit-moistened eyes
and ask: *What country are you from?*

Translation by David Allen Sullivan and Dr. Abbas Kadhim

Ode to the Little "r"

Aracelis Girmay

Little propeller
working between
the two fields of my a's,
making my name
a small boat
that leaves the port
of old San Juan
or Ponce,
with my grandfather,
Miguel, on a boat,
or in an airplane,
with a hundred or so
others, leaving the island
for work, cities,
in winters that would break
their bones, make old,
old men out of all of them,
factory workers, domino
players, little islands themselves
who would eat & be eaten by Chicago,
New York, the wars
they fought without
being able to vote for
the president. Little propeller
of their names: Francisco,
Reymundo, Arelis, Margarita,
Hernán, Roberto, Reina.
Little propeller of our names
delivering the cargo of blood
to the streets of Holyoke,
Brooklyn, New London,

Ojai, where the teacher says,
"Say your name?" sweetly,
& the beautiful propeller
working between
the two fields of my a's
& the teacher saying, "Oh!
You mean, 'Are-Raw-Sell-Lease.'"
Or "Robe-Bert-Toe"
or "Marred-Guh-Reetuh, like
the drink!" & the "r"
sounding like a balloon
deflating in the room, sad
& sagging. I am hurt.
It is as if I handed her
all my familiar trees & flowers,
every drawing of the family map
& boats & airplanes & cuatros
& coquis, & she used her English
to make an axe & tried to chop
them down. But, "r," little propeller
of my name, small & beautiful monster
changing shapes, you win. You fly
around the room, little bee, upsetting
the teacher & making all of Class-310A laugh,
you fly over the yard, in our mouths,
as our bodies make airplanes over the grass,
you, little propeller, are taking over the city,
you are the sound of cars racing, the sound
of bicycle spokes fitted with playing cards
to make it sound like we are going fast,
this is our ode to you, little "r," little
machine of our names, simple
as a heart, just working, always,
there when we go to the grocery,
there in the songs
we sing in our sleep.

Madame Intuita

Izabella Morska

My whole life's like learning a second language—
so many immigrant sacrifices but in the end
I can't get rid of this accent, recognized
everywhere to my annoyance.
And I'd been feeling almost assimilated!
All that effort, and for what?

Overwhelmed by the mystery of it,
I enroll in a class of heightened conversation.
There I also speak with an accent—
even more pronounced—and sometimes lose
whole threads or connections. It can't be helped.

You could call this a 'mother tongue'
but I don't have a mother, only a handful
of old wives' tales and myths: watch the distracted
woman dancing on a tightrope—will she fall?
will she find something to grab onto?
The careful charting of her mood swings
doesn't exactly encourage fluency.

That other language, elusive yet familiar, is like water:
slips through my fingers, empty
but for a trace of dampness, an aftertaste
of crystalline pleasure. In the meantime,
like an early Renaissance poet,
I savor the elaborate undergirding of Latin
with its praiseworthy logic.

The language of the educated classes
gives me an edge in rhetorical contests.
But in a weak moment, I neglect all
those sensible rules, and my background is suspect.
One can blot out the past with intense effort
but it will never fully disappear.

Unsure of myself, I stop speaking altogether
and just try to make out sounds—
a mountain stream spilling onto a valley of rocks
disappears like a shaky pulse, an echo,
an elf—now you hear me, now you don't—
and before I can laugh, I'm up to my knees
in layers of hurt and shame. How to wade through?

Elsewhere I come upon fragments of letters, stories broken off.
I tie up those loose ends, restore lines with my pen.
I'm content, I only look, I don't say a thing—
don't dare to breathe so as not to frighten
that roadside creature half-woman, half-beast.
When I turn around and look that way again
will I glimpse at least a print from her tiny hooves?

Translation by Karen Kovacik

Our Neighborhood in Revere, MA:
Circa 1984 and 2008

Bunkong Tuon

Listen, you have seen it before
in countless movies and TV shows.
No matter which city
you're talking about,
the markers are the same:

The sneakers on telephone wires,
the cracked sidewalks, the potholes
that you swerve so hard to avoid
that you almost hit the double-parked cars,
the graffiti on street signs and public buildings,
the apartment complex and family
houses slumped so close together that you can smell
your neighbor's fried pork with rice,
where you can taste the lemongrass, fish sauce,
red chilies, and brown golden garlic,
as if your grandmother is cooking next door,
where inside, English is not spoken,
and the first image greeting you might not be Christ,
where you need to lift up the reservoir's lid and pull the string
to flush the toilet,
where a grease-encrusted can of Sanka filled with brown Canola oil
rests near the stove,
where if you pay careful attention, you will notice that there are other
inhabitants besides your friend's extended-extended family,
and across the street, you hear a bunch of young men
hanging out on the front porch of a house with broken windows,

you see air-conditioner on the brown grass,
and you notice a mother walking down the sidewalk,
with some of her children running ahead of her,
and another one, a baby in only a diaper,
and not because it's summer hot, cradled to her chest.

You have seen it on the ten o'clock local news.
A young reporter staring wildly into the camera
is speaking with a sense of authority
and commitment to the community,
about a shooting that claimed the lives of young bystanders,
about a drug bust where police found some untold
amount of coke and drug paraphernalia,
and you are shaking your head,
wondering what the world has come to, now
that these foreigners are ruining our America.

I was in the neighborhood the other day
with my fiancée.
Fresh from graduate school, studying
postcolonial literature and theory, we were
there to pick up some curry for my aunt.
I scan, trying to get a sense of the scene,
making sure the car doors are locked.
The streets, the smells, the sights reminded me
of the old neighborhood, the markers were there,
but the people that I knew were gone.
Now there were Middle Easterners.
I guess the United States is no longer at war
with Southeast Asia.

Cell Phones Burning

David Morse

A woman on a cell phone talks insurance
to seed-flats full of broccoli and marigolds.
Behind sunglasses, she is elsewhere. Sun
fills the pale murky sky, air pungent as spit
on a hot light bulb, from fires raging half
a planet away, at St. James Bay or
the Mexican plains or the dying
rain forests of the Amazon basin.

Something is happening. Not here, never
here, but somewhere. Not an eclipse or coup.
Not in Nairobi or New York. But somewhere
men in business suits with box-cutters and
coins for eyes are spamming babies, cutting
the heart out of places *like this*, carving
villages into fast food until nothing is left
but bulldozers leaking rust under this pale
sky and discarded numbers ticking.

Pierre Joris

death toll of foreign soldiers in 2010 to
166 in Afghanistan
McLaren driver Jenson Button won the
Chinese Grand Prix
re-open the skies over Europe
ash from a volcano in Iceland
a high pressure here and a low pressure
there
News broke that an explosion occurred at 11
p.m. EST on BP's Deepwater Horizon oil rig
in the Gulf of Mexico southeast of Venice
the jet stream came down, spun around, &
then went back up through the Straits of
Gibraltar
amphibians, reptiles, mammals, bird and
fish species
Remembering Columbine 11 years ago
celebrate National Park Week
largest subtropical wilderness
showdown Senate financial reform
Zephyrs top Express in 11 innings
Today's Money Word is deflation
BIG Oil Rig Explosion Off Louisiana Coast,
11 to 15 People Missing, Infernal Blaze
trust leaked away with the Tritium
bar NEPA analysis of climate change impact
Being fat is bad for your brain
erratic, potentially fatal heart rhythms
defibrillator responsibility the Guidant
Corporation

short-circuit and fail
"Nobody is being held accountable."
Google criticized privacy practices
the privacy rights of the world's citizens
forgotten
stricter enforcement of title IX
Twain's last words
Best Non-holiday Quarter for Apple
Taliban sniper fire lethality rates drop
Peter Steele "Life is killing me" is dead
no ban on animal cruelty videos
Off Louisiana Coast, 11 to 15 People
Missing,
Statoil Committed to Oil Sands
Bush warcrimes on off Broadway
Miami Condo Sales rise
Oil Rig Explosion Infernal Blaze
boxer hangs himself in jail
Reds pitcher Volquez suspended
Tuesday, April 20
News broke that an explosion occurred at 11
p.m. EST
on BP's Deepwater Horizon oil rig in the
Gulf of Mexico
52 miles southeast of the Louisiana port of
Venice.
According to the Coast Guard, 11 to 15 crew
members were reported missing
of the total 126 workers aboard the rig
at the time of the blast.

Estimated Prophet: Version

The second angel poured out his bowl into the sea, and it became
blood like that of a dead man; and every living thing in the sea died.
—Revelation 16:3

Geoffrey Philp

The prophets have abandoned us to our lies.
They've packed spare clothes, retreated to the Mojave
Where they can still bless wild, untamed spaces,
Praise the elation of kestrels, their aerial dance
Away from smoke that poisons the brave,
Threads a man's lungs and veins with fine lace,
Sweetens a mother's milk that darkens her firstborn's eyes:
Rattlers coiled under a Joshua tree have a better chance.
And it's no use begging like televangelists for them to come
back
Who'd want to listen on the "burning shore" anyway?
Everyone knows true holy lands are far across the sea
And you can't tweet prophecy any more than you can save
Pelicans from the spray of dispersants or mangroves from an oil
slick.
No, better to mortgage our dreams. At least, that's what the
voices say.

Patient

Greg Delanty

The snow has melted clean off the mountain.
     It's winter still. Yet another indication that Gaia
is in trouble, that things aren't sound.
     The rocky mountain top shines
like the bald head of a woman after chemo
     who wills herself out of her hospital bed
to take in the trees, the squirrels, the commotion
     in town, sip a beer in a dive, smile
at the child ogling her shiny head, wishing
     it didn't take all this dying to love life.

Depleted Uranium

Teresa Mei Chuc

The water runs
a neon color
in the village.

All the villagers
know why
the babies

are born dead
and deformed.

Others say
there is no
proof it was
the war.

Sometimes
truth can
only be
understood:

the father carries
the little body
wrapped in a
blanket.

She will be buried
with a wooden
grave marker,

her name
inscribed
with a knife.

The war
in
Afghanistan
began in 2001

and one day
the U.S. will
leave there

in the soil
in the water
for generations...

There are coffins
that are only
six inches long.

If you place
your hand
inside,
it will fit.

Laren McClung

one

The scar runs down his stomach exactly the width of a child's
thumb. In the summer I would trace the smooth river of skin
dividing his torso into hemispheres, his navel surgically moved
to the right. Inside wires hold the muscles in place. His small
intestine, half-removed, & what's left has been routed through
the abdomen & sutured to his side. *Agent Orange*, he says & I
picture a man in a prison uniform, or a swami wearing a robe
that symbolizes fire & the burning of ego, or Christo's *Gates*
swaying through the city, the color of caution, & opposition.

two

I am four. He has to undergo another operation. What I remem-
ber is him standing in the dining room. He hands my mother an
envelope. He's wearing a gray shirt. His hair has just been cut.
Her hands shake as she takes the money from him. Three weeks
later in the hospital his blue robe moves slowly down the hall, an
IV rolling at his side.

three

When his hair grew back from the chemo, it was dark & thick
& curly, my mother tells me. & then, *You know he doesn't shit
from his asshole.* She laughs when she says it.
Because he hung a sword in the living room, left a machete
under the mattress, danger was a synonym for father, & for sum-
mer. One night my mother slept, or had not slept, a .45 pressed
into the small of her back. The Stones played on an old cassette.

PART 5:

DRUMS IN
THE NIGHT

Coaching Winter Track in Time of War

W. D. Ehrhart

The boys are running "suicides"
on the football field today:
ten-yard increments out to the fifty
and back again, push-ups in between.
It's thirty degrees, but they sweat
like it's summer in Baghdad,
curse like soldiers, swear to God
they'll see you burn in Hell.

You could fall in love with boys
like these: so earnest, so eager, so
ready to do whatever you ask,
full of themselves and the world.

How do you tell them it's not that simple?
How do you tell them: question it all.
Question everything. Even a coach.
Even a president. How do you tell them:
ask the young dead soldiers coming home
each night in aluminum boxes
none of us is allowed to see,
an army of shades.

You tell the boys "good work" and call it a day,
stand alone in fading light while
memory's phantoms circle the track
like weary athletes running a race
without a finish line.

Torsion

Yusef Komunyakaa

He was in waist-high grass. An echo of a voice
    searched for him as he crawled along a ditch,
the greenhorn's blood reddening the mud, & the scent
    of burnt Cosmoline. *What's the spirit of the bayonet,*
soldier? His mind the mouth of a cave, the horizon
    was nitrate as he walked on his hands,
a howl in the crosshairs, rain tapping his helmet.
    He had been tapered, honed & polished in AIT,
& then pointed toward grid coordinates on a ragged map,
    his feelings cauterized, & now a glint of wet light
touches the sniper's rifle in a grove of jackfruit.
    Silence, a stone in his belly, an anvil on his head.
What's the spirit of the bayonet, soldier? He dove on the pig
    & his body became part of the metal, tracer rounds
scorched the living air, the dirt & sky, & the edges of night
    approached. Only his fingers would recall threading
another belt of ammo. He didn't wish to know how many
    shadows hugged the ground. No, he couldn't stop
firing as he rode the M60 machinegun to a primal grunt
    before he buckled & spewed vomit over the barrel,
the torsion a whiplash of hues. *What's the spirit*
    of the bayonet, soldier? After medevac choppers
flew out the badly wounded & the body bags,
    three men in his squad became two tigers at sunset
& walked through the village. They kicked a pagoda
    till it turned into the crumbly dust of cinnabar,
& then torched thatched roofs. The captain's citation
    never said how fear tussled him in the paddy ditch,
& the star in its velvet-lined box was a scarab
    in a pharaoh's brain. The dead visited nightly.

The company chaplain blessed him, but he'd sit hours
        gazing out at the sea & could never bless himself.
The battalion saluted but he wished to forget his hands,
        & the thought of metal made him stand up straight.
He shipped back to the world only to remember blood
        on the grass, men dancing on a lit string of bullets,
women & children wailing among the flame trees,
        & he wished he hadn't been trained so damn well.
What's the spirit of the bayonet, soldier? He was back
        now, back to where he brandished fronds as swords
to guard their tree house, his mama at church
        singing hallelujah, his daddy in Lucky's
swigging Falstaff. He kept thinking of his cousin Eddie
        who drove his girl to Galveston in a Chevy pickup,
"California Dreaming" looping through the cab.
        He could still see round fishing boats on the edge
of the South China Sea, a woman's long black hair
        falling in a rising wave, moonlight on the skin
of sappers, their bodies wound in concertina.
        He switches off his blue transistor radio
& walks straight into pines along the Black Warrior,
        searching for arrowheads, bagging rabbit & quail.
He's back to the Friday his draft card came, when he first
        mastered a willful blindness, back to outsmarting prey,
& he duck-walks across the clearing under power lines.
        Now ashamed of something naked as a good question
redbirds flash in a counter ambush. *Thou shall not kill*
        echoes across clay hills miles from his loved ones,
& he slouches deeper into the Choctaw's old growth,
        through a hoop of light, away from a face stealing
his brother's, so deep he can hardly hear himself plead
        to shiny crows in a weeping willow.

Written in Red Tears

Vuong Tung Cuong

A gentle glance -
glint of mountain rain,
light on sea

The river Lam -
its shores eroded
sails - destroyed by bombs

In the army, he followed
a phosphorescent light
into the dark night
chaos and struggle
gun in hand

many times
nearly dying
and dying

But now, in his hands are
a pen and an injured heart

Blood and fire from the war
become trickles of ink
in long nights

Words drop like sugar water,
bringing back to life
the destroyed forest

Perfumed incense burns
at Dongloc Thre junction

Burning the gloom
into warmth,
trust and love

Humans are more human
after profound suffering and misfortune.

I imagine him
in a small house
in ancient Hanoi
a strong wind blows
through a side window

Silent and alone

Hair white as smoke
candle light during the unending night
On the desk, white papers throb
like silver moonlight on the river Lam

a red tear drops from pen
onto paper
and is absorbed gently

Translation by Teresa Mei Chuc and Tran Huy Quang

The Sound of Drums in the Night

Dau Phi Nam

The sound of drums in night
cleaved to sleep

Hand around an egg,
around a rice bowl -

Birth-death, death-birth
A fragile human life

How many more
bones on the battlefield
drumming - the sound of battle
reaches the blue sky
clouds glide
rows and rows

Thousands of years remain
Majestic monuments

Tung...tung... farewell
Nameless ancient tomb
Eternally blue grass

Zhaojun sings plaintively
"The song of a warrior's wife"

Translation by Teresa Mei Chuc and Tran Huy Quang

Song of Napalm

for my wife

Bruce Weigl

After the storm, after the rain stopped pounding,
We stood in the doorway watching horses
Walk off lazily across the pasture's hill.
We stared through the black screen,
Our vision altered by the distance
So I thought I saw a mist
Kicked up around their hooves when they faded
Like cut-out horses
Away from us.
The grass was never more blue in that light, more
Scarlet; beyond the pasture
Trees scraped their voices into the wind, branches
Crisscrossed the sky like barbed wire
But you said they were only branches.

Okay. The storm stopped pounding.
I am trying to say this straight: for once
I was sane enough to pause and breathe
Outside my wild plans and after the hard rain
I turned my back on the old curses. I believed
They swung finally away from me ...

But still the branches are wire
And thunder is the pounding mortar,
Still I close my eyes and see the girl
Running from her village, napalm
Stuck to her dress like jelly,

Her hands reaching for the no one
Who waits in waves of heat before her.

So I can keep on living,
So I can stay here beside you,
I try to imagine she runs down the road and wings
Beat inside her until she rises
Above the stinking jungle and her pain
Eases, and your pain, and mine.

But the lie swings back again.
The lie works only as long as it takes to speak
And the girl runs only as far
As the napalm allows
Until her burning tendons and crackling
Muscles draw her up
Into that final position

Burning bodies so perfectly assume. Nothing
Can change that; she is burned behind my eyes
And not your good love and not the rain-swept air
And not the jungle green
Pasture unfolding before us can deny it.

The Truce

Patricio Manns

The glow of a cigarette flickers out there
Smoke floats up and dies as it rises
Among the grasses, I hear sobbing
Because this is not peace
It's barely a truce

The air reeks of the stench of war
As I write over my rifle
perhaps my last love letter to you
I don't want your pain
I don't want your pain
But today I felt its shadow

Napalm is not the only truth
Nor is the cannon
My whole being wants to escape the cruel
Obligation
Of killing someone
I never knew
I never knew

Today I suddenly remembered my childhood:
I saw the blue sky, the bygone times
My brother in the sun, running through cornfields
While here we spent our days killing

Tell who you want that he deserted
That he went far away, that he won't be coming back.
I will look for the flower he never found.

The flower of truth
And place it on the ground where he lies

The only truth is a great
Brotherhood
My hand rejects the mortal
Resignation
Of firing on someone
I never knew
I never knew.

The glow of a cigarette flickers out there
Smoke floats up and dies as it rises
Among the grasses, I hear sobbing
Because this is not peace
It's barely a truce

Translation by Joanne Pottlitzer

A Memory of Language

(América en el idioma de la memoria)

Gioconda Belli

I've heard my ancestors' language in dreams.
I've seen them in the dim light of strange rooms
which I can only name in the foreign language
of those who forever confined them
to the region of shadows.
I can't understand their words
but in the dreams they rise like palm trees
and shimmer like Quetzal feathers.
What were the markets like in *Tenochtitlán*
the cry of the feather-sellers announcing macaw tufts
the voice of the woman offering *quequisque* or *yuca*
the somber voice of the potato merchant?
With what words like rivers or rain
did the hero of the sacred ball game
and the gentle girl with the *jipijapa* baskets
declare their love to one another?
The words of a people resemble their mountains and lakes
resemble their trees and their animals
What were the sounds of this language
that spoke of *ceibos* and jaguars
of an incandescent and equatorial moon
of erect volcanoes?

I have heard the language of my ancestors
In dreams
In strange rooms which I can only describe
in the language of destruction.

They ravaged us.
But we hid our Gods, our myths
under the purple mantles of their saints.
We took their language and made it ours.
We brought into it the sounds of torrential rains
and the sweet laments of the *quena*
the wind at the height of the Andes
and the impenetrable jungle of the Amazon.
To survive we let them change our names
But we named the world
with codes and codexes they still cannot decipher.
We shed our old skins.
With cacao we anointed their genes
to bring forth light chocolate and burnt chocolate.
Chocolate men and women populating anew
the continent of Thunder and Desolation.
We rebuilt our magnificent cities
Mexico, Buenos Aires, Lima, Rio
and we preserved in the deepest of our earthen jars
the wisdom of our trampled memory.

Who are we?
Who are these men, these women without words
mocked for their color
their feathers and adornments?
So that we would not read but their codexes
they burnt ours on tall bonfires
Our history, our poetry, the annals of our peoples
became smoke in our eye-sockets
and filled our entrails with tears.
Flames consumed the *amates* so carefully painted by our scribes.
Flames consumed the stories that made us what we were.
How the elders howled in the squares
seeing the names of their forebears ablaze.
Oh, long night, sad night of ashes
Night in which we were left without hands, without words,

without memory,
turned into slaves, sleepwalkers.

Earth, blood, the color of fruits saved us;
the wind sweeping through the gorges of Macchu Picchu.
They took everything but Earth kept singing to us
Iguazu's Falls, Titicaca, the Orinoco, the Pampa,
Atitlan, Momotombo, Tikal, Copán
Earth knew the touch of our hands
the volcanoes spoke to us, the rivers washed our tears
the jungle gave us a hiding place.
They were consumed by nostalgia. Gold extracted its price.
They killed each other. Their boats sank.
Their children didn't recognize them.
They became extinct in our women's wombs
Their genes boiled in the cacao
and they could no longer
recognize themselves in their descendants,
in their brown-skin, straight hair children.

I've heard the language of ancestors
In dreams
In dreams I've heard their laughter.
There's a patience that patience breeds,
resilience.
We have waited a long time.
For centuries we have waited.
The flux of time rises spiraling
from the deserts in Patagonia
across the Andes, the mountain ranges, the rain forest
the buffalo plains.
In the large cities men destroy their world
Hunger, dispossession dig tunnels beneath their feet
erode the foundations of their beliefs.
The poor have their hope.

Earthen vessels where water is kept,
a memory of grief.

The America of our elders awaits the return of Quetzalcoatl
the plumed serpent.

I've heard the language of my ancestors
In dreams
Dreams that never sleep.

Translation by Charles Castaldi and Natasha Hakimi

Guatemala 1988

J. Patrice McSherry

what are the reasons?
he asked, with
brown eyes immobilizing

me in a smoky
stare, eyes that told
of Latin dreams

hates and angers.
a chill
like the grasp

of a wind
its serrated edges
raking the skin

and he asks
how do you explain
your people?

and words die
in a jungle
of black nights

split by fire
where men with no names
whisper

and wait, until dawn
when villages stir
and then the screams from the

sky tear the haze
and one more child
is dead, one more

woman, two more farmers.
or the men with
no names

who wait in city streets
as the doctor locks
the door

behind him,
turning the key
and turning

into the bright light of blood
of frozen
tomorrows, of bullets.

the bullets are American
he says
and eyes burning

and words
failing, the reasons
are like sticks

in the winds of a hurricane.

Such is the choquero

Jorge Montealegre Iturra

Black like the coal of Lota,
the raven and the mouth of a cannon.
Such is the choquero,
good and bad
like the one that inhabits the Mississippi.

Blackened
by the beautiful fire
that lights up the night
that embraces and scorches
        (that consumes little by little
        the wood that was tree,
        the tree that gave fruit,
        the fruit that was ours).
Black friend
craved for by the fraternal bonfire,
valuable blackish brooch
of the passionate lady
of glittering sparks and stars.

Such it is,
happy and sad.

Blackened
under a bridge of the Mapocho
awaited by the child and the dog,
the children's poverty
and the hungry bark
that expect from you,
choquero,

your vital and nutritional warmth,
with a taste of home and family
…home that vanishes
in the evasive steam
of your sad mouth.

Faithful choquero
of the break of a sweaty day's work,
of a proletarian breakfast

and the quarter kilo of bread
trick of the salaried hunger.

Yes, such it is:
poor and poor.

Inseparable companion
of the adventurous wanderer,
you are guitar and wandering sandal,
humble walker
of the path
that roaming travels.

Chacabucan choquero
inhabitant of the cold kitchen,
of the melancholic flame,
of the cooking stove without a woman.
Quiet witness
of sad privacy
that one drinks sip by sip
with nostalgia and rage.

Such it is
imprisoned and free.

Choquero you make possible
the coffee chats,
the circle of bitter mate
the home present in the memory,
the choca while strumming the guitar
the hot aguita of hope
that boils every day
in the choquero of history.

Such it is:
black,
happy and sad,
poor,
free and imprisoned.

Such is the choquero.

The Colonel Comes Calling

Bill Tremblay

A black sedan, gleaming chrome grill
sidled   stopped   no din, just
the zzz of a right rear window sliding down,
a dead fish voice Siqueiros recognized
from the revolution. He bent in half to look inside.
Salazar in his Chief of State Police uniform.

David climbed into the Colonel's web on wheels.
—*To the Electricians' Union Building, the uniform told his driver.*
Siqueiros grinned.—*Is there anything you don't know about me?*
The unmarked Buick carved the rotary.
The Angel of Independence reached up,
holding the promissory note for heavenly rewards,
yet trapped by one toe in its terrestrial prison.

The Colonel offered a cigarette.—*Still interested in politics?*
He flamed both cigarettes with a gold lighter.
Siqueiros opened an ash tray in the door,
—*You've been ghosting me since I got back from Spain.*
The Colonel's eyebrow raised slightly.
—*Maybe you should have stayed there.*
Then you wouldn't be pursuing the fantasy
that your god-like artistic powers will free
         the poor-in-spirit from their gloom.

Banks flashed stock quotes in digits.
It's Friday, the clocks said.
Traders were taking profits from teachers' pensions,
from farmers' children, buying houses
they planned to burn to the ground.

They knew how to make money from disasters.
They had bought insurance.

Hundreds of file clerks, all aluminum elbows,
knees, silver spiked high heels, black plastic
umbrella rapiers, crowded into skyscrapers,
the scythes of their mouths grim as they steeled
themselves to turn humans into "data."
—*Is this the change we fought for?*
The Colonel sneered.—*We fought for pocket change.*

Along the Paseo men in gray jump-suits
swept sidewalks with palmetto brooms between
busts of Mexico's heroes and royal palms.
—*The way the workers get screwed never changes.*
Siqueiros reached, took the Colonel's
sunglasses off, startled to see an eight-year-old
in military costume, epaulets, medals, hat dwarfing him.
His brushy eyebrows looked glued on.
Siqueiros fought back a smile as he watched
the boy Salazar lift his cigarette to his little mouth.
—*Please, no rants,* he squeaked.
Just don't go to the march against Trotsky.

Sun sliced his eyes through the still-opened window.
—*What march?*
—*Don't play stupid, David.*
The Colonel put his sunglasses back on.
Siqueiros saw reflected in the Colonel's mirrors
himself as a young Captain on a troop train
with machine-guns chugging north to Sonora.
1919. Locomotive steam, Cigarette smoke.
The Mexican time-machine.
Monte Alban's stone gods. Oaxaca's church spires.

Sunlight glittered on the Colonel's medals, epaulets.
—*Let me paint your portrait. You're ready now.*

At the corner of Insurgentes a traffic cop
in leather jacket, jodhpurs, white helmet, wrote
a ticket with quetzal pen on a white-haired cabbie,
who, hands together, prayed, fervent to be let off.
—*A pitiful sight, a man with no palanca,* the Colonel observed.
But as a hero of the revolution you could write your own ticket
            if you'd just …
—*That's exactly what I must not do, Leandro.*

The car slowed to a red light stop.
Beggar women held their babies in their arms.
David quick opened the Colonel's door, jumped out,
and, as a *collectivo* swung by, jumped on,
flipping his cigarette out that hit
the Buick's windshield in a disaster of sparks.

The Eyes of Korea

Wilson Powell

I wanted to escape
the eyes of POWs
hunkered down
resting from filling sandbags
staring quiet hate at me.
I was afraid, dismayed
shakily indignant
what had I done to them?

The old man's eyes
told me nothing
as he stood under his huge
A-frame load of sticks
waiting for me to decide
if he was enemy or not.
Did he care? I couldn't tell.

The smiling prostitute's
wrinkles overran her face
without touching the eyes.

Contempt, brutality
hard-cored the
National Police Lieutenant's
otherwise artless eyes.
He liked our trucks
hated our drivers
pursued his graft in secret.

He gave me a big, big smile
after shooting his own
sleeping guard.

The eyes over the prisoner's
split, swollen cheekbones
flashed helpless rage
with each impact
of the Police Lieutenant's
gloved and weighted hand;
stoically dulled
at the questions in between
closed altogether
when he passed out.

A young soldier
killed his first enemy
then talked too much,
eyes convulsing
as fear and triumph
relief and shame
took turns battering his future.

The sergeant's eyes were tired
when he told him,
"The choice wasn't yours.
Forget it."

Another soldier's eyes looked within
at spectres unimaginable
as he tried to tear away his face
from shame, just shame.
My arms tired
holding his down all night
compassion stretched
from talking reason

to the unheeding ears,
of a casualty
who would receive no Purple Heart.

Two boys frozen together
in each other's arms.
I couldn't see the eyes
I knew were in there
looking at their last dreams.

One boy,
hands on stolen wood
to build his hut,
stood wide-eyed, paralyzed
trembling until half way through
the heated C-ration.
Then he smiled
all the way up to his eyes.

The farmer's eyes,
humbly shadowed
under downcast brow,
were warmly grateful
shaming us who could only bring
money and things to support
his compassion for orphaned children.

I wanted his eyes to find mine.

Habeas Corpus

America, 2012

Tyehimba Jess

You have the body, ankle and hip, each parted lip and each hair,
the body with its sweatstained heat and its cough, the spleen and
tongue of the body is yours from navel to spine. You have the
body bundled like a fist, shuddered in darkness, bound, bloodied,
under suspicion. You have the body blistered with accusation:
hooded, blinded, manacled, maced. You have the body electrified,
born unto the body of the republic we stand in stress position.
You have the body numbered, targeted, locked, firing sequence
initiated, search warrant expired when you have the body
expired, exploded, the body preening in the wedding party, in a
car speeding through night, in the morning before prayer, trial
held in the head of the soldier flying bodiless remote drone from
his body. I am the body in this voice in my silence the body rots
the body unwilling to answer when you have the body and the
blood on the body you have. The body stretched and water-
logged, named and unnamed, foreign and domestic, accusation
in the eye of the body plucked out you have the body shipped
into concrete and photographed stripped. You have the skull and
the penis and the heart of the body, each vulva and opening, the
digital record of the body as it writhes. You have the body defin-
itively indefinitely, the body huddled in the shape of our body,
the body you have is the body you have. You have the body.

Ripping off morality and the Timorese

Vacy Vlazna

In a plane above Rai Timor
two swine robbin' the maubere blind
swilled champagne
clinked to piracy
toasted occupation
saluted aberrations
cheers to genocide mate!

Far below, in a death net of military
camps, prisons and checkpoints
cut from the outside world, cemeteries burgeoning,
lay the Land of Crosses tilled by
bony dead men-women-children walking
who'd never heard champagne pop!

Poor little Timor *Loro Sai* bordered
by parasites, pragmatists, assassins
and the usual fence sitters
(staring the other way because
the sight of so much blood may offend)
Santa Cruz, Deir Yassin, My Lai, El Mozote, Rwanda,
Falluja, what an etcetera mess!
Fear not your friends will not forget you
ha ha ha pigs fly
clink clink let's drink to that!

ouroboros

woorabinda, central queensland

Paul Summers

beware the magi bearing gifts;
their votive grog & lavish guilt.

the former, laced; the latter,
the spike. shame & the shame

of shame. death & the death of
death. the snake will bite its tail;

& these mothers, their tongues.
a silence forged, a flawless edge

to hamstring progress. the birds
have flown. the kangaroos have

seen the light. the brumby bolted
to the downs. three score years &

ten of drought & flame, of blood &
shit congealing on this bitter earth.

PART 6:

EYES WIDE
OPEN

Important Things Happen

Gerardo Guinea Diez

I look out the window
/air and lightness
it seems I'm on the other side of things

days full of radio and bad news
Wall Street and its miracle men clamor
about the good business climate
/outside, only curses

I close my eyes and dream
/in seconds
History sways on its handrail:
the deportation of Gypsies
the massacre of migrants in Mexico
millions unemployed
/hunger placed on the table

it's the same speaker
/or the same story?
I break the window before anyone
can shout: things look better than ever before

the phone rings
/women are talking in the hallway
about birds and fashions
I pick up the receiver
/fix my gaze
a familiar voice is tangled
with an absurd story
I listen to it for a while:

Bakunin and his stay in Carrara
/a story about anarchy, I realize.

I'll find a way to go on
/vaguely the air filters
through the broken glass
like an inescapable fact

the radio dramatizes then gasps
/a voice explains the plot:
the wrathful god of the Bible
will send
signs:

rains
Pakistan, China, Central America
beneath the waves

hurricanes
/the Caribbean standing on bones of solitude

tsunamis
—Japan and its world of dew—

men with nooses around their necks
death, on deck, sails the great seas

heat waves
/hegemony of sand

—without doubt,
important things will follow—

Translation by Erica Mena

A Bird's Nest in Gezi Park

Müesser Yeniay

I am writing these words from a bird's nest
between two branches, in Gezi Park
like a knife my breath is stuck in my chest
they are coming to destroy the sky
a sky filled with all the people of the earth

I'm in a bird's nest in Gezi Park
between two branches

here the people are poisoned
the trees uprooted

we are being expelled from
where our mothers invited us

they are bombing the songs of birds
(birds cannot produce the sound of cash)

Ethem is heard, a simurg in fire!
A welder's body in Ankara
is collapsing like a feather
they are grinding us into dirt before we die
under smoke street children and cats...
on their bent backs a lost dream
one cannot look at the world with blind eyes...
or fall to sleep in an unexpected moment!
in an unexpected moment, to sleep...

I am in a bird's nest in Gezi Park
between a pair of branches

Desert Spring

For those who took to the streets in Oman and paid with
their freedom as a price for our freedom, this whisper is for you.

Ali Saif Al Rawahi

The kiss between the crimson blood and
The gray asphalt quickened the sand
Drops of sweat painted the picture with purity
The air carried the roaring sound; eagles soaring above echoed it eagerly
The sun gazed in confusion
Nothing seemed to disturb the eternal stillness of this desert
They camped on the edge of immortality
And at the gates of glory opened wide their chests for the black arrows
Of hate and ignorance
Injustice they have slaughtered, inequality they have demolished
Into the ashes they have planted the seed of freedom
It will take time to grow but once its roots are enveloped by
The earth-soul, it shall be there to stay
You have started a hurricane that will sweep out the flowers of evil
Be proud
You have set a great fire that will burn down the poisonous pillars of tyranny
Be proud
You have opened minds and awakened souls and implanted hope
Be proud
A candle cries in the face of darkness
Only by freedom, is freedom obtained

What is to Give Light

Yahia Lababidi

What is to give light must endure
burning, a man once said
Another man became the matchstick
that set a nation aflame

But fire, and its appetite, cannot be
calculated, like freedom
Injustice and desperation make men
combustible, like dry wood

When words lose their meaning
and an entire people their voice -
so they can neither laugh nor scream-
death and life begin to taste the same

From Tunisia, to Egypt, to Lebanon to Yemen
the light from a burning man proved catching
And those with nothing to lose, or offer, but bodies
fanned the embers of their hopes into a blazing dream.

Your smile is sweeter than the national flag

To Sanaa

Taha Adnan

Your mobile's dead
your landline's not responding;
on Facebook your picture's gone away,
the national flag draped down
over your smile,
over the gleam in your eyes.

I move along the wall: your wall,
I scrutinize it, clicking and updating,
I brush from it the dust of grief
and stillness.
The clouds above the country could clear;
the wall might split open
on your captive face.

As though it truly mattered
I brooded fretfully and add it up:
has revolution swept the land?
Has spring, a whirlwind, passed through
for your absence to flourish
in autumn?
Or have I missed the train
only to remain right here:
an indifferent witness?

I lit up Al-Jazeera
where coddled Arabs
set revolutions ablaze

in sister states,
frame hearts
and impetuous scenarios
and compose ad lib laments
sung by a turbaned chorus
to the strains of an orchestra coached
to mourn.

Nothing new in Arabism:
killing is the order of the day
and blood up to the knees.

There, on the revolution's stage
tragedy is comedy,
rulers are vampires
and the people a clutch of fools
careening after a tattered rag
they think a flag
and like a crowd of extras
chanting: "The people want…"

With trembling fingers I pick up
the remote
and put out the revolution
your smile might flutter in my mind
and rally, sleepwalking, to your banner.
You are my flag and my revolution
and I am your loving people,
your beloved leader.

I take up the receiver
(the heart wants it so):
your mobile's dead
and your landline's ringing,
Ringing…but no answer.

On Facebook
the homeland's colours hide
your smile.

Your smile is sweeter
than spring,
than all the seasons;
your smile is more magnificent
than the crowds in full cry,
more radiant than the people when they rise up
and sing, "My country";
your smile, a joy
at every gathering,
your smile, God's protection settled
within my heart,
your smile—
O beat of my heart—
exalted above every banner,
sweeter than the national flag.

Translation by Robin Moger

Lionel Fogarty

Love ... walk with me
Love ... waken with me
Love ... is a black newborn
Camp fringe dwellers are my love
Love is not seen in cities
Love is my Father
Love is my Mother
Scrubs are hid in bush love
And we say
Love's mine.
Love is alive and received.
Love is a kangaroo
Love is an emu
Love is the earth
Love is the love of voice
Love is my friend.
And what about us?
Well, love smells.
Us Murris knows
It's love in bad love.
Give us love. Give us love.
Our Dreamtiming is love.
Catch my love over a fire
Fire of love.
Culture is our love.
Culture is ourself in love.
The school won't give you love
So we black power give you love
Proud and simply
Love is the love

To our lands love.
Love walk with me
Love awaken with me
Now give us the true love.

Stop Me Like Blood

Dimitri V. Psurtsev

The warrior has lain here a long time.
Though his side is still warm,
He lost consciousness
Three hundred years ago.
Stop me like blood,
Lick me, so that I don't spill
From his warm side, pierced
With the spear of fate.
(And Fate, having pulled out
Its spear, shakes its shield
Like the fearsome goddess Athena,
And snow leaves the banks,
Filling the world with silence,
And along the road the fir trees
Sleep, their black wings folded).
I ooze his delirious speech
Invisibly in the air of the fields.
Stop me like blood.

Translation by Philip Metres

13 ways of looking at the towers
(a 9/11 poem, 10 years later)

(with all due respect to wallace stevens)

Evie Shockley

i.

among twenty deadly
catastrophes, the only thing
that moved us
was the felling of the towers.

ii.

we were triple-stricken
with grief, as if
we had lost three towers.

iii.

the towers flamed in the summer sky.
they were little flickers in the light show.

iv.

the north tower and the south tower
were one.
the north tower, the south tower, and the freedom tower
are one.

v.

i do not know which amazes me more,
the outpouring of international sympathy
or the outpouring of nationalist rage,
the white-hot ash still sifting through the air
or just after.

vi.

news media filled the tv screens
with instant replays.
the shadowy airplanes
crossed them, o'er and o'er.
our mood
sought in the shadows
a blameworthy cause.

vii.

o stout men of washington,
why do you imagine an axis of evil?
don't you see the proud towers
lying in rubble around the feet
of the bankers of manhattan?

viii.

we know manifest destiny
and a century of economic domination;
know, too,
that the towers are involved
in what we know.

ix.

when the towers cascaded to the ground
it marked the end
of one of many mythologies.

x.

at the sight of the new tower
revising the blue-gold horizon
even the most disaffected of americans
would gasp fiercely.

xi.

we rumbled over baghdad
in armored tanks.
there, a loneliness crushed us,
in that we mis-equated
the toppling of the dictator's statue
with the felling of the towers.

xii.

the muslims are praying.
the tower must be standing.

xiii.

there was oppression in all the democracy.
we were dying
and we were going to die.
the tower spun up
another story.

Eyes Wide Open

Sam Hamill

The little olive-skinned girl
       peered up at me
from the photograph

with her eyes wide open,

deep brown beautiful eyes
       that bore silent witness
to a grief as old as the ages.

She was young,
       and very beautiful, as only
the young can be,
       but within such beauty
as bears calamity silently:

because it has run out of tears.

I closed the magazine and went
       outside to the wood pile
and split a couple of logs, thinking,
       "Her fire is likely
an open fire tonight,
       bright flames licking
and waving

like rising pennants in the breeze."

When I was a boy,
       I heard about the bloodshed
in Korea, about the Red Army
         perched at our threshold,
           and the bombs
that would annihilate our world

forever.

I got under my desk with the rest of the foolish world.

In Okinawa, I wore the uniform
       and carried the weapon
until my eyes began to open,
       until I choked
on Marine Corps pride,
       until I came to realize
just how willfully I had been blind.
How much grief is a life?
       And what can be done unless
we stand among the missing, among the murdered,
       the orphaned,
our own armed children, and bear witness

with our eyes wide open?

When I was a child, frightened of the night
       and crying in my bed,
my father told me a poem or sang,

"Empty saddles in the o-l-d corral,
where do they r-i-d-e tonight."

Homer thought the dead arrived
       into a field of asphodels.

"Musashino," near Tokyo, means
      "Musashi's Plain,"
the warrior's way washed in blood.

The war-songs are sung
      to the same old marching measures—
oh, how we love to honor the dead.

A world without war? Who but a child or a fool
could imagine such a thing?

Corporate leaders go to school
      on Sun Tzu's Art of War.
"We all deplore it," the President says,
      issuing bombing orders,
"but God is on our side."

Which blood is Christian,
which Muslim, Jew or Hindu?

The beautiful girl with the beautiful sad eyes
      watches, but
has not spoken. What can she

possibly say?
      She carries the burden of finding
another way.

In her eyes, the ruins, the fear,
the shoes that can't be filled, hands
that will never stroke her hair.

But listen. And you will hear her small, soft, plaintive voice
—it's already there within you—
a heartbeat, a whisper,

a promise broken—
if only you listen

with your eyes wide open.

Notes on the Title and Selected Poems

The Title

The phrase "With Our Eyes Wide Open" derives from the title of the final poem in the anthology. Thanks to Sam Hamill for permitting West End Press to base our title on his poem, "Eyes Wide Open."

"Poems of the New American Century" is also a borrowed term. *Life* magazine publisher Henry Luce published an article titled "The American century" in 1941, as America was about to enter the Second World War. The subtitle also recalls a manifesto issued in 2000 by the Project for the New American Century, a Washington, D.C. think tank, proposing how America could expand its global military dominance. The manifesto suggested that transforming America into a bastion of conservative values would be a long process, "absent some catastrophic and catalyzing event—like a new Pearl Harbor."

The anthology begins with Martin Espada's poem "Alabanza: In Praise of Local 100," which is dedicated to the 43 members of Hotel Employees and Restaurant Employees Local 100 who lost their lives in the 9-11 attack on the World Trade Center. The next selection, "The Nobodies" by Eduardo Galeano, sets the tone for the remainder of the anthology, by moving the narrative away from the 9-11 terror attack on the United States, and focusing it on the people of the world whose suffering so often escapes notice. Through varying situations and stories within the collection, the reader moves within this distressing reality. The collection ends with Sam Hamill's poem, "Eyes Wide Open," picturing a "girl with the beautiful sad eyes" who "carries the burden of finding/ another way."

Section 1: Alabanza

Daisy Zamora was a combatant for the FSLN (Sandinista National Liberation Front) during Nicaragua's Sandinista Revolution. She became the voice and program director for clandestine Radio Sandino during the final 1979 Sandinista offensive, then vice minister of culture for the Revolutionary government.

Wanda Coleman's jazz-influenced "American Sonnets" were inspired by the unrhymed blank verse sonnets Robert Lowell began in the late 1960's.

Lionel G. Fogarty dedicated his poem "For I Come – Death in Custody" to his brother Daniel, who died in police custody in 1993. Fogarty is a member of Murri people who inhabited modern-day Queensland, Australia, before the European occupation. A corroboree is a sacred ceremony during which the Aborigines interact with the Dreamtime through dance, music and costume. Dreamtime is held to be an ancient, sacred era in which ancestral totemic spirit beings created the world.

Lesego Rampolokeng said of the woman in his poem: "Not one woman, but most of the women I grew up with and who raised me share that experience, or some such. My sister was dragged naked through the Soweto streets one Christmas."

Jazra Khaleed in his poem "Words" refers to Mustapha Khayati, who published an essay titled "Captive Words: Preface to a Situationist Dictionary" in 1966, in which he claimed that "criticism of the dominant language, its détournement, will become a permanent practice of the new revolutionary theory."

Rethabile Masilo's poem "The Boy Who Would Die" is dedicated to his nephew, Motlatsi Masilo. "He died in his sleep," Masilo explained, "at three years old when the bullets meant for my father found him instead. Our home was attacked in September 1981 by "unknown" assailants in the early morning hours. Motlatsi was the only one who died that day."

Makhosazana Xaba refers in her poem to Moeketsi James "Stompie" Sepei, a teenage African National Congress (ANC) activist, who was found dead on December 29, 1988. One of Winnie Mandela's bodyguards was convicted of his murder. Xaba was a member of the African National Congress (ANC) in Moscow for military training when she was first informed of Stompie's death.

Section 2: love at a distance

Phillippa Yaa de Villiers is a South African of mixed Australian and Ghanaian ancestry. Although the US supported the white minority Apartheid government and deemed the African National Congress a terrorist organization, many South Africans were inspired by the American Civil Rights movement and, later, the election of Barack Obama.

Bratislav Milanović, in his poem "A Whistle Over Belgrade," recalls the day in May 1999, when NATO bombed a residential area in Belgrade, ostensibly to destroy a military target. The US called the bombing of Yugoslavia, which lasted from March 24, 1999 to June 10, 1999, "Operation Noble Anvil."

Phomolo Lebotsa's poem "Resigned to my karma" tells about Lesotho's oppressive textile industry. Lesotho is a country within South Africa.

Samah Sabawi's poem "A Confession" tells about Israel's military assault, Operation Cast Lead, which began without warning on 7 December 2008 and ended on 18 January 2009. 1400-1500 Palestinians were killed, including approximately 300 children. Gaza was utterly devastated. Perhaps a dozen Israelis died in the conflict.

Lia Tarachansky's poem "Poem for Samah" is a response to "A Confession." Habibti means "my love" and is a popular term of endearment Palestinians use with close friends and loved ones. As Tarachansky explains, "Here I also use it because it is often times the only Arabic word Israelis know, except the orders we're taught in the army, like "Iftah el bab" meaning "open the door" and "jibel hawiyah" meaning "give me your ID." We don't really speak the Palestinians' language or hear their stories."

Section 3: Jumping Jack

Teresa Mei Chuc's poem concerns the M16 Mine, an anti-personnel mine used by American forces in Vietnam. It was designed for use in open spaces. When tripped, a small charge launched the mine a few feet in the air, where it detonated and sprayed fragmentation horizontally, about waist-high. Many of these unexploded bombs remain in Vietnam.

Sabah Mohsen Jasim in "Inanna Moaning" refers to Inanna, a prominent female deity in ancient Mesopotamia. Her name means "Queen of Heaven." Lamassu is a Babylonian deity with a human head, five legs, and huge eagle wings.

Philip Metres in "The Iraqi Curator's Power Point" recalls the invasion of Iraq in 2003 by US forces, and their failure to guard the museum. "During the chaos that followed," Metres noted, "thousands of antiquities were stolen from the famed Iraq National Museum in Baghdad; though some key pieces have been returned, thousands remain lost."

Elena Fanailova's poem "...Again they're off for their Afghanistan" concerns the invasion of Afghanistan by Soviet forces in December 1979 on behalf of Afghanistan's government, which was battling Muslim forces backed by the US. Soviet forces on their way to Afghanistan often passed through Grozny, the capital city of the Chechen Republic, and Ashkhabad, the capital city of Turkmenistan. Soviet forces remained in Afghanistan until 1989. "The Hep" is hepatitis.

Section 4: Cell Phones Burning

Rafiq Kathwari said about his poem: "Two of the three India-Pakistan wars were over Kashmir - the first in 1947-48 and the second in 1965. The de facto border dividing Kashmir between India and Pakistan is one of the most militarized boundaries in the world. Tens of thousands of troops face each other across the 460-mile Line of Control. The line has been a source of conflict for almost the entire period of existence of India and Pakistan."

Pierre Joris noted that "Wordswarm 20 April 2010" concerns the BP Gulf "Deepwater Horizon" oil spill disaster. His sequence of poems was commissioned by The Crossing, Donald Nally conductor, for their Month of the Moderns 2013, with Funding from the Pew Center for Arts & Heritage through the Philadelphia Music Project.

Geoffrey Philp's poem "Estimated Prophet: Version" derives from a Grateful Dead song (words by John Perry Barlow, music by Bob Weir) covered by Burning Spear.

Section 5: Drums in the Night

Vuong Tung Cuong's poem "Red Tears" was inspired by the novels *Red Tears* and *Girls of Dongloc* by Tran Huy Quang. Vuong Tung Cuong is a North Vietnamese veteran of the American War.

Dau Phi Nam's poem "The Sound of Drums in the Night" refers to "bones on the battlefield," a line taken from the poet Tao Tung. The person in his poem, Zhaojun, lived in the Chien Quoc era. To bring about a truce in the war, Zhaojun was to be given as tribute to the Ho dynasty. In the legend, the grass on the Ho land was totally white, but on Zhaojun's grave, the grass was blue all year long. "The song of the warrior's wife" is the long poem by the 17th century Vietnamese woman poet Doan Thi Diem.

Patricio Manns wrote his poem "The Truce" about the Tet truce, a brief ceasefire during the lunar New Year in South Vietnam.

Gioconda Belli's poem "A Memory of Language" refers to several noteworthy places and things. Tenochtitlán was an Aztec city-state located on an island in Lake Texcoco in the Valley of Mexico. Jipijapa is a palm-like plant. Ceibos is a tree with lovely red flowers. Quena is a flute used by people in the Andes. The gorges of Macchu Picchu are in Peru. Iguazu's Falls are on the border of the Brazilian state of Paraná and the Argentine province of Misiones. Titicaca is a large lake in the Andes on the border of Peru and Bolivia. Atitlan is a large lake in the Guatemala highlands. Tikal is one of the largest archaeological sites and urban centers of the pre-Columbian Maya civilization, in Guatemala. Copán is the site of Mayan ruins in Honduras.

J. Patrice McSherry's poem "Guatemala 1988" refers to US intervention in Guatemala. In modern times, the CIA staged a violent coup in Guatemala in 1954 on behalf of US corporate interests, and the US sided with the forces of repression against progressives from 1960 through 1996, during Guatemala's civil war.

Jorge Montealegre's poem "Such is the choquero" first appeared in 'Chacabuco 1973' (a bulletin board of political prisoners in the prison camp Chacabuco) in 1974. Since then it has been published in various books and magazines, but never in any of his books. It has been put to music by Payo Grondona. Several words and phrases in the poem should be noted. Lota was a coal mine in the south of Chile; it is symbolic of the conditions of exploitation of the miners. The Mapocho River crosses Santiago, the capital of Chile. Many street children live below its bridges. Chacabucan derives from Chacabuco, a former nitrate mine that in 1973 was converted into a prison camp, where the poet was incarcerated. Mate is a type of bitter herb tea drunk in the Southern Cone. It is often passed around and shared within a circle of friends. Choca is a meal or drink consumed in a choquero (jar). Agüita is a diminutive of water.

Bill Tremblay's poem "The Colonel Comes Calling" is about Mexican muralist David Siqueiros, a life-long Communist and hero of the Mexican Revolution (1910-1920).

Vacy Vlazna said about her poem: "Just as Blair can't shake off the Iraq gorilla clinging to his back, Australia's former Minister for Foreign Affairs and Trade, Gareth Evans, will forever be Indonesia's apologist who helped steal East Timor's oil resources." Rai means Land. Maubere means the people. Timor Loro Sai is East Timor.

Section 6: Eyes Wide Open

Gerardo Guinea Diez's poem "Important Things Happen" refers to Mikhail Alexandrovich Bakunin (1814 – 1876), a Russian revolutionary and founder of social anarchism philosophy. He is known for having organized trade unions and workers' organizations around the world.

Müesser Yeniay's poem "A Bird's Nest in Gezi Park" was written while she participated in the 2013 Gezi Park protests in Turkey. The initial protest was staged in opposition to an urban development plan for Gezi Park in Istanbul, but additional protests spread across Turkey after the forceful eviction of the protesters. Protests continued for several months and came to encompass many human rights issues. Ethem was a man killed in the protests. A simurg is a mythical flying creature, resembling a phoenix.

Ali Saif Al Rawahi's poem "Desert Spring" is about the protests that began in Oman in February 2011. Initially peaceful, the protests turned violent. The Sultanate of Oman is an absolute monarchy of nearly four million people. The US has three major military bases in Oman. It signed free-trade agreement with Oman in 2009, and several American oil companies operate there, including Halliburton and Occidental.

Yahia Lababidi's poem "What is to Give Light" was inspired by the Egyptian Revolution and was composed two days into the uprising. "What is to give light must endure burning" is an often quoted line by Austrian psychiatrist and Holocaust survivor Victor Frankl. The lines, "Another man became the matchstick/ that set a nation aflame," refers to Mohamed Bouazizi of Tunisia, whose act of self-immolation ignited the Tunisian Revolution, the Egyptian Uprising, and the Arab Spring.

Taha Adnan's poem "Your smile is sweeter than the national flag" refers to Al-Jazeera, a media outlet based in Qatar, focusing largely on Arabic political news. Facebook is an internet social website used during the Arab Spring for organizing political action.

Lionel Fogarty said: "My writing is to give a direction to Aboriginal people coming up in the future, to stay away from European colonialist ways of writing, and the disease of stupidity in their language. I want to use a method encouraging the readers to accept that the solitary Aborigines write to give spiritual and political understanding of the conventional social structure of their community."

Dimitri V. Psurtsev said about his poem "Stop Me Like Blood:" "The almost-slain warrior of the poem is Russia, emanating delirious speech/literature/poetry. The classical reference to Athena has to do with the fact that our fate was to inherit the so-called Hellenism from the Greeks, and also that even our Gospel was translated from the Greek."

Acknowledgments

Taha Adnan, "Your smile is sweeter than the national flag," translated by Robin Moger, in *Banipal* 46 (April 2013). Reprinted with the permission of the author.

Ali Saif Al Rawahi, "Desert Spring" [previously unpublished]. Copyright © 2014 by Ali al Rawahi. Reprinted with the permission of the author.

Tahar Bekri, "Afghanistan" from *The Parley Tree: Poets from French-speaking Africa and the Arab World*, edited and translated by Patrick Williamson (ARC Publications, 2012). Reprinted with the permission of the author.

Gioconda Belli, "Memory of Language," adapted by Gioconda Belli and Charles Castaldi from a translation by Gioconda Belli and Natasha Hakimi. Originally published in *Mi intima multitude* (Visor, 2007). Reprinted with the permission of the author.

Metin Cengiz, "At War," translated by Müesser Yeniay. Reprinted with the permission of the author and translator.

Floyd Cheung, "Names of the Dead" from *New Verse News* (December 3, 2009) and "Names of the Dead II" from *New Verse News* (December 14, 2009). Reprinted with the permission of the author.

Teresa Mei Chuc, "Jumping Jack: The M16 Mine" (previously unpublished). Copyright © 2014 by Teresa Mei Chuc. "Depleted Uranium" from *Hypothetical Review 1* (2013). Both reprinted with the permission of the author.

Wanda Coleman, "American Sonnet (210)" from *Mercurochrome*. Copyright © 2001 by Wanda Coleman. Reprinted by permission of Black Sparrow Books, an imprint of David R. Godine, Publisher, Inc.

Dau Phi Nam, "The Sound of Drums in the Night" from *Hoa sim (Myrtle Flower)* (Hanoi: The Woman Publisher, 2010). Reprinted with permission of the author and translator.

Greg Delanty, "Patient" from *The Greek Anthology, Book VII*. Copyright © 2010, 2015 by Greg Delanty. Reprinted with the permission of Louisiana State University Press and Carcanet Press, Ltd.

Gerardo Guinea Diez, "Important Things Happen," translated by Erica Mena [translation previously unpublished]. Originally appeared as "Este poema forma parte" from *País con lunita* (Costa Rica: Editorial Germinal, 2013). Reprinted with the permission of the author and translator.

Linh Dinh, "Rueful Outlays for a Conscript" from *Jam Alerts* (Tucson, Ariz.: Chax Press, 2007). Copyright © 2007 by Linh Dinh. Reprinted with the permission of the author.

W. D. Ehrhart, "Coaching Winter Track in Time of War" from *The Bodies Beneath the Table*. Copyright © 2010 by W. D. Ehrhart. Reprinted with the permission of the author and Adastra Press.

Martín Espada, "Alabanza: In Praise of Local 100" from *Alabanza: New and Selected Poems 1982-2002*. Copyright © 2003 by Martín Espada. Used by permission of the author and W. W. Norton and Company, Inc.

Elena Fanailova, "...Again they're off for their Afghanistan" from *The Russian Version*. Copyright © 2009 by Elena Fanailova. Reprinted with the permission of Ugly Duckling Presse.

Lionel G. Fogarty, "For I Come – Death in Custody" and "Love" from *New and Selected Poems* (Melbourne: Hyland House, 1995). Copyright © 1995 by Lionel G. Fogarty. Reprinted with the permission of the author.

Eduardo Galeano, "The Nobodies," from *The Book of Embraces*, translated by Cedric Belfrage with Mark Shafer. Copyright © 1989 by Eduardo Galeano. Translation copyright © 1991 by Cedric Belfrage. Used by permission of the author and W. W. Norton & Company, Inc.

Aracelis Girmay, "Ode to the Little "r"" from *Kingdom Animalia*. Copyright © 2011 by Aracelis Girmay. Reprinted with the permission of The Permissions Company, Inc., on behalf of BOA Editions, Ltd, www.boaeditions.org.

Eliza Griswold, "Ruins" from *Poetry* (December 2012). Reprinted with the permission of the author.

Sam Hamill, "Eyes Wide Open" from *Measured by Stone* (Curbstone Press, 2007). Originally published in *Rattle 25*

Contributor Notes

Taha Adnan grew up in Marrakech and has lived in Brussels since 1996. A poet and writer, he co-edited the *Moroccan Poetry Journal* (*The Poetic Attack*) in the 1990s. The year 2003 saw the publication of his first collection of poems by the Ministry of Culture in Morocco. Adnan has headed the Brussels Arabic Literary Salon since 2005. His poems have been translated into French and Spanish and published in Lebanon, Morocco, Belgium, and Costa Rica.

Ali Saif Al Rawahi was born in 1983 in Muscat, Sultanate of Oman. He holds a Bachelor Degree in English Literature and studied in the United States as part of a US-sponsored exchange program. His poems have been published in the US in the anthology *Sunflowers and Seashells: Days Remembered* (Eber & Wein, 2011). He has won several literary competitions including a first place in novel writing in 2009 from the Literary Society in Oman.

Adnan al-Sayegh was born in al-Kufa (Iraq) in 1955. He is one of the most original voices from the generation of Iraqi poets known as the Eighties Movement. In 1993 his uncompromising criticism of oppression and injustice led to his exile in Jordan and Lebanon. After being sentenced to death in Iraq in 1996, because of the publication of *Uruk's Anthem*, he took refuge in Sweden. Since 2004 he has been living in London.

Tahar Bekri was born in Tunisia in 1951 and has lived in Paris since 1976. He writes in both French and Arabic and is considered by critics among the important contemporary North African poets. He has published over 30 works, and has been translated into several languages. His poetry evokes the continual reinvention of East and West. It is preoccupied by exile and wandering, at the crossroads of tradition and modernity. He is currently Maître de conférences at Université de Paris Ouest-Nanterre.

Gioconda Belli is a Nicaraguan poet and novelist. Her books *The Country Under My Skin, The Inhabited Woman, The Scroll of*

Seduction and *Infinity in the Palm of Her Hand* have been translated into English. Her poetry has won numerous prizes in Spain and Latin America.

Metin Cengiz was born in Göle in 1953, and graduated from Erzurum Atatürk University, Department of French, in 1977. He lives in Istanbul where he works as a proofreader, editor and translator at publishing houses. He established the Digraf Publishing House in 2005, in collaboration with his friends, to publish poems and essays concerning poetry theory. He won the Behçet Necatigil Poetry Award in 2006 with his book Şarkılar Kitabı (*The Book of Songs*), and the Melih Cevdet Anday Poetry Award in 2010.

Floyd Cheung is associate professor of English Language and Literature and of American Studies at Smith College. Born in Hong Kong, he grew up in Las Vegas, earned his B.A. at Whittier College, and his Ph.D. in English at Tulane University. His poems can be found in such journals as *Mascara Literary Review*, *qarrtsiluni*, and *Rhino*.

Teresa Mei Chuc was born in Saigon, Vietnam, shortly after the horrendous war that bombed her people and her homeland. Nominated for a Pushcart Prize for "Truth is Black Rubber," a section of poems from *Red Thread*, Teresa Mei Chuc is a graduate of the Masters in Fine Arts in Creative Writing program at Goddard College in Plainfield, Vermont, and teaches literature and writing at a public school. Her poems appear in journals including *EarthSpeak Magazine*, *National Poetry Review*, *Rattle*, and *Verse Daily*.

Vuong Tung Cuong was born in 1950 in Habac Province, Vietnam. He is a veteran, reporter and poet. He has published nine collections of poetry. Cuong lives in Dalat city.

Wanda Coleman was a Guggenheim fellow, Emmy-winning scriptwriter, former columnist for Los Angeles Times magazine; a nominee for poet laureate, California 2005 and for the USA Artists Fellowship 2007. Coleman's books from Black Sparrow (Godine) include *Bathwater Wine*, winner of the 1999 Lenore Marshall Poetry Prize (Coleman was the first African-American woman to receive the award), and *Mercurochrome* (poems), bronze-metal finalist, National Book Awards 2001.

Greg Delanty's latest book is *So Little Time*, Green Writers Press. His next collection *Book 17* is due from Louisiana State University Press in Spring, 2015. Other recent books are *Loosestrife*, Fomite Press; *The Word Exchange, Anglo-Saxon Poems in Translation*, WW Norton; and his *Collected Poems 1986-2006*, Carcanet Press. He has received many awards, most recently a Guggenheim for poetry. He teaches at Saint Michael's College, Vermont.

Linh Dinh was born in Vietnam in 1963 and came to the US in 1975. He is the author of two books of stories, five books of poems, including *Jam Alerts* (2007), and a novel, *Love Like Hate* (2010). His work has appeared in numerous anthologies and has been translated into many languages. He is also the editor of *The Deluge: New Vietnamese Poetry* (2013). He has been tracking the deteriorating socialscape through his frequently updated photo blog, State of the Union.

W. D. Ehrhart, a Marine Corps veteran of the Vietnam War, teaches and coaches at the Haverford School in suburban Philadelphia. He is the author or editor of 21 books of poetry and prose.

Martín Espada was born in Brooklyn, New York in 1957. He has published more than fifteen books as a poet, editor, essayist and translator. His latest collection of poems, *The Trouble Ball* (Norton, 2011), is the recipient of the Milt Kessler Award, a Massachusetts Book Award and an International Latino Book Award. His work has been widely translated. A former tenant lawyer, Espada is a professor in the Department of English at the University of Massachusetts-Amherst.

Elena Fanailova is a Moscow poet. Born in Voronezh, she holds degrees in medicine and journalism; she worked for six years as a doctor at Voronezh Regional Hospital. In 1995 she became a correspondent for Radio Svoboda, and moved to Moscow in the late nineties. Her poetry often explores issues of politics, ethics, sexuality, and violence, as in the poem reprinted here. She has won the Andrei Belyi Prize and has published six books of poetry.

Lionel G. Fogarty was born in 1958 on the Cherbourg Aboriginal Reserve. He is a Murri man, poet and activist. His first collection of poems, *Kargun*, was published in 1980, and he has since published eight further collections. Since the 1970s he has been active in many of the political struggles of the Aboriginal people, from the Land Rights movement, to the issue of Aboriginal deaths in custody.

Eduardo H. Galeano (1940) is a Uruguayan journalist, writer and novelist. His best known works *Memory of Fire Trilogy*, 1986 and *Open Veins of Latin America*, 1971, have been translated into 20 languages and transcend orthodox genres: combining fiction, journalism, political analysis, and history. He said about himself: "I'm a writer obsessed with remembering, with remembering the past of America above all and above all that of Latin America, intimate land condemned to amnesia."

Aracelis Girmay is the author/collagist of the picture book *changing* (Braziller, 2005) as well as the poetry collections *Teeth* (Curbstone Press, 2007) and *Kingdom Animalia* (BOA Editions, 2011). She currently teaches at Hampshire College.

Eliza Griswold lives in New York City. She is the author of a collection of poems, *Wideawake Field* (2007) and a non-fiction book, *The Tenth Parallel: Dispatches from the Fault-line between Christianity and Islam* (2010), which was awarded the Anthony J. Lukas Prize in non-fiction. Both books are published by Farrar, Straus and Giroux. Her book of translations, *I Am the Beggar of the World: Landays from Contemporary Afghanistan*, will be published in April 2014, by Farrar, Straus and Giroux.

Gerardo Guinea Diez is a poet, novelist and journalist. In 2000 he received the Cesar Branas National Poetry Award. In 2006 he won the Luis Cardoza y Aragon Mesoamerican Poetry Award for his book *Poemas para el martes* (*Poems for Tuesday*). In 2009 Letra negra (Black Letter) published his collection of poems *Casa de nosotros* (*Our House*). In 2012 his collection *Cierta grey alrededor* was a finalist for the Rubén Darío International Poetry Award.

Suheir Hammad is an award winning poet raised in Brooklyn, NYC. Her works include *Born Palestinian, Born Black* (Harlem River Press, 1996), *Drops of This Story* (Harlem River Press, 1996), *Zaatar Diva* (Cypher Books, 2006), and *breaking poems* (Cypher Books, 2008).

Sam Hamill is the Founding Editor of Copper Canyon Press and the Founder of Poets Against War. His *Almost Paradise: Selected Poems & Translations* was published in 2005. A collection of his poetry, *Habitations: Selected Poems*, will be published by Lost Horse Press in September 2014.

Lance Henson is a Cheyenne dog soldier poet living in self-exile in Italy. He has published 42 books of poetry in 25 languages. He is a member of the Native American Church, the American Indian Movement. He has participated in the Southern Cheyenne Sundance for over 20 years as both dancer and painter.

Sabah Mohsen Jasim was born in Iraq in 1951. He has been published widely in Iraq. He received a Certificate of Honor as a participant in the San Francisco International Poetry Festival, July 27-29, 2007. He has had two books published in Serbia: *Premonitions Far of Memory* (poetry collection) and *That Wild Flower* (short stories). Sabah translated Lawrence Ferlinghetti's book *Poetry as Insurgent Art* into Arabic, and the book will soon be published and distributed in Iraq.

Tyehimba Jess is a Detroit native. His first book of poetry, *leadbelly*, was a winner of the 2004 National Poetry Series. *The Library Journal* and *Black Issues Book Review* both named it one of the "Best Poetry Books of 2005." Jess, a Cave Canem and NYU Alumni, received a 2004 Literature Fellowship from the National Endowment for the Arts, and was a 2004-2005 Winter Fellow at the Provincetown Fine Arts Work Center. Jess is an Assistant Professor of English at College of Staten Island.

Pierre Joris is a poet, translator, essayist & anthologist. Recent publications include *Meditations on the Stations of Mansur al-Hallaj* (poems) and *The University of California Book of North African Literature*, coedited with Habib Tengour. Forthcoming are *Barzakh—Poems 2000-2012* (Black Widow Press) and *The Collected Later Poems of Paul Celan* (Farrar, Straus and Giroux).

Rafiq Kathwari, a Kashmiri-American rebel poet who lives in New York City, is grateful that his work has found a home at the literary blog *3QuarksDaily*. He is the winner of the Patrick Kavanagh Poetry 2013 Award, the first non-Irish to win in the 46 year history of the award.

Jazra Khaleed was born in 1979 in Grozny, Chechnya. He lives in Athens' inner city and writes poetry in Greek, publishing mainly in samizdat and online. He edits the literary magazine *Teflon*, in which he publishes his own poems, translations and essays. His poems have appeared in distinguished magazines, such as *World Literature Today, Modern Poetry in Translation, Westerly* and *Die Horen*. He is co-publisher and editor of Topovoros Books, a small publishing house located in Exarchia, Athens.

Yusef Komunyakaa has published 17 books of poetry, including *Neon Vernacular*, which won the Pulitzer Prize. In addition to poetry, Komunyakaa is the author of several plays, performance literature and libretti, including *Saturnalia, Weather Wars, Testimony*, and *Gilgamesh*, which have been performed in venues including the 92nd Street Y in New York City, Opera Omaha in Nebraska, and the Sydney Opera House in Australia. He is a Professor and Distinguished Senior Poet at New York University.

Adrie Kusserow is professor of cultural anthropology and chair of the Department of Sociology and Anthropology at St. Michael's College in Vermont. She is co-founder of Africa Education and Leadership Initiative: Bridging Gender Gaps Through Education. Her poems have been published widely in journals such as *The Kenyon Review, Harvard Review, Prairie Schooner* and *Best American Poetry*. Her most recent book of poems entitled *Refuge* was published by BOA Editions, Ltd. in 2013.

Yahia Lababidi is the author of five well-received books in four different genres: *Signposts to Elsewhere* (aphorisms), *Trial by Ink: From Nietzsche to Bellydancing* (essays), *Fever Dreams* (poems) and

The Artist as Mystic (conversations). His latest book, a collection of short poems, *Barely There*, was recently featured on NPR.

Phomolo Lebotsa was born in the late 1970s. His connection with Black sound and rhythm might also emanate from echoes of past Sunday mornings - with his father playing Jazz on the family Pho stereo. An unpublished writer of poetry that sings from the heart, Phomolo wants to tell stories of hope and triumph. He lives in Berea, Lesotho with his wife and son, where he tries to build bridges between business, art and sports.

Valerio Magrelli (Rome, 1957) is the author of five poetry collections and four books of prose, for which he has won numerous prizes. A Professor of French literature at the University of Pisa and then Cassino, he is also a frequent contributor to the cultural pages of several Italian dailies. His poems have been translated into English, French, Spanish and a number of other languages.

Patricio Manns has developed an extensive body of work as a novelist, essayist, poet, and playwright. He is one of the most important members of the New Chilean Song Movement and continues to perform and compose extensively. After the military coup in 1973, he lived in exile in France until the end of the 1990s. In 1988 he won a Guggenheim Fellowship in Literature, and his books have won many other awards since then.

Hugh Martin grew up in northeast Ohio and served six years in the Army National Guard as an M1A1 Tanker. He deployed to Iraq in 2004 and later graduated from Muskingum University. Martin is the author of the chapbook, *So, How Was the War?* (Kent State UP, 2010) and *The Stick Soldiers* (BOA Editions Ltd., 2013), which won the A. Poulin Jr. Prize. Martin has an MFA from Arizona State and is currently a Stegner Fellow at Stanford University.

Rethabile Masilo is a Mosotho poet currently living in Paris, France with his wife and two children. Thirty-three years ago he fled his home country, Lesotho, with his family and moved through South Africa, Kenya and the United States. He has been published internationally in numerous journals and magazines, and his first poetry collection, *Things That Are Silent*, was published by Pindrop Press in 2012.

Laren McClung is the author of *Between Here and Monkey Mountain* (Sheep Meadow Press). Her work has appeared in reviews including *The Massachusetts Review*, *Cerise Press*, *The American Reader*, *PN Review*, and *War, Literature and the Arts*. She has offered writing workshops to residents at Goldwater Hospital on Roosevelt Island, and to veterans of the wars in Iraq and Afghanistan. She is co-editor of the anthology *Inheriting the War*, and currently teaches at New York University.

J. Patrice McSherry is Professor of Political Science and founding Director of the Latin America and Caribbean Studies Program at Long Island University, New York. She has won awards for her books, teaching, and research on Latin America. She has written poetry since adolescence, some of which has been published; one of her poems won an award in 1990.

Sarah Menefee is a long-time homeless rights activist, an active member of Occupy San Francisco, and a founding member of the League of Revolutionaries for a New America and the Revolutionary Poets Brigade. Her latest collections of poetry are *Human Star* and *In Your Fish Helmet*.

Philip Metres has written a number of books and chapbooks, including *A Concordance of Leaves* (Diode 2013), and *abu ghraib arias* (Flying Guillotine 2011), winner of the 2012 Arab American Book Award in poetry. His work has garnered two NEA fellowships, the Thomas J. Watson Fellowship, five Ohio Arts Council Grants, the Beatrice Hawley Award, the Cleveland Arts Prize and the Creative Workforce Fellowship. He is professor of English at John Carroll University in Cleveland, Ohio.

Dunya Mikhail, Iraqi-American poet, was born in Baghdad in 1965 and came to the US (Michigan) in mid 1990s. Her first book in English, *The War Works Hard* (New Directions 2005, Carcanet 2006) was shortlisted for the Griffin Prize and was named one of the 25 books to remember in 2005 by the New York Public Library. Her *Diary of A Wave Outside the Sea* (New

Directions, NY, 2009) won the 2010 Arab American Book Award.

Bratislav Milanović is a Serbian poet who has published eleven poetry collections and one novel. A selection of his poems entitled *Doors in a Meadow* has been published in the US (Lewiston: The Edwin Mellen Press, 2011). Milanović has been a member of the Association of Writers of Serbia and Serbian PEN. He has won the National Award for Outstanding Contribution to the Culture of the Republic of Serbia. He lives in Belgrade with his wife Verica and son Vladislav.

Jorge Montealegre is a Chilean journalist, teacher, poet, and scholar of cultural studies, especially themes of memory and graphic humor (doctorate in American Studies from University of Santiago de Chile). He was imprisoned at Chacabuco by the Pinochet regime in 1973. He has authored numerous books of non-fiction and poetry, and won many literature and poetry awards.

David Morse's themes involve human rights and environmental issues. One of a handful of journalists to visit South Sudan in 2005, he returned to Sudan in 2007 with support from The Pulitzer Center on Crisis Reporting and The Nation Institute's Investigative Fund. His poetry has appeared in *Blue Collar Review*, *California Quarterly*, and *Tiger's Eye*, among many others. His poems are featured in *Embark*, published in 2012 by Toadlily Press. He is also author of a novel, *The Iron Bridge* (Harcourt Brace, 1998).

Izabela Morska (b.1961) authored the collection of poems, *Madame Intuita* (2002), as well as numerous works of prose and the full-length drama *Księga Em* [*The Book of M*], based on the life of the transgender writer Maria Komornicka. From 2003-2006, she held a visiting position at the University of California at Berkeley. She currently teaches American literature and culture at the University of Gdańsk.

Dau Phi Nam was born in 1965 in Nghean Province, Vietnam. He has a PhD in medicine. His poems appeared in the weekly poetry magazine, *Vannghe Vinh*. He lives and works in Nghean city.

Pina Piccolo is a bilingual Italian-American cultural activist and poet who writes, now mostly in Italian, about a variety of topics including immigrant rights, decolonization processes , resistance movements, women's rights, and environmental concerns. She has been active in the 100 Thousand Poets for Change movement, mainly in the Bologna area, publishes almost exclusively online, and contributes regularly to Italian language online literary journals.

Geoffrey Philp, author of *Bob Marley and Bradford's iPod* and spokesperson for the Coalition for the Exoneration of Marcus Garvey, teaches English at Miami Dade College. A critically acclaimed author, he has also won many awards for his poetry and fiction, including a Florida Individual Artist Fellowship, the Sauza "Stay Pure" Award, and James Michener Fellowship from the University of Miami. In 2008, Philp won the "Outstanding Writer" prize from the Jamaica Cultural Development Commission.

Paul Polansky (born 1942 in Mason City, Iowa) is an expatriate-American writer who has lived in Europe since 1963 and brought out more than 40 books with European publishers. Polansky drew international attention in the 1990s with his books about Lety, a WW II Roma (Gypsy) death camp run by the Czechs for the benefit of a local nobleman. In 2004 he was awarded the celebrated Human Rights Prize of the city of Weimar. His books have been widely translated.

Wilson Powell was born in Cambridge, MA, in 1932. He was raised in Ohio and California. He is a Korean War veteran, USAF, 1950 to 1954. He has pursued careers in publishing, construction and steel industry sales, and hazardous materials management. He is founder of the Gateway Society of Hazardous Materials Managers, the largest chapter of the Academy of Hazardous Materials Managers, a certifying professional organization. He served as Executive Director of Veterans For Peace, 2001-2005.

Dimitri V. Psurtsev is a Russian poet and translator of British and American writers and poets. His two books of poetry, *Ex Roma Tertia* and *Tengiz Notepad*, were published in 2001. He teaches translation at Moscow State Linguistic University and lives with his wife Natalia and daughter Anna outside Moscow.

Lesego Rampolokeng was born on July 7, 1965 in Orlando West, Soweto. He is the author of ten books of poetry and prose, as well as several audio-recordings. He has collaborated with numerous musicians. He has directed several documentaries focusing on human rights issues.

Margaret Randall (born in New York in 1936) lived for a quarter century in Latin America and returned to the US in 1984 only to be ordered deported for the content of some of her books. She won her case in 1989. Her most recent books include: *As If the Empty Chair / Como si la silla vacía; The Rhizome as a Field of Broken Bones* (poetry, Wings Press); and *Che On My Mind* (a feminist poet's reminiscence of Che Guevara, Duke University Press). Randall lives in Albuquerque and travels widely to read and lecture.

Samah Sabawi is a writer, political analyst, commentator, author and playwright. Her articles and poetry have appeared in various publications. She is co-author of *Journey to Peace in Palestine* and writer and producer of the plays *Cries from the Land, Three Wishes*, and *Tales of a City by the Sea.*

Tim Seibles, born in Philadelphia in 1955, is the author of several poetry collections. His latest book, *Fast Animal*, was one of five poetry finalists for the 2012 National Book Award. A National Endowment for the Arts fellow, Tim's poetry is featured in several anthologies. He is visiting faculty at the Stonecoast MFA in Writing Program sponsored by the University of Southern Maine. He lives in Norfolk, Virginia, where he is a member of the English and MFA in writing faculty at Old Dominion University.

Aharon Shabtai is one of the Hebrew language's leading poets, as well as a translator of Greek drama into Hebrew. He has published some 20 books of poems, and English translations of his poetry have appeared in numerous journals, including the *American Poetry Review*, the *London Review of Books*, and *Parnassus: Poetry in Review*. Shabtai is an outspoken critic of Israeli policies in the Palestinian territories, and of human rights violations against Palestinians.

Solmaz Sharif is currently a Wallace Stegner Fellow in Poetry at Stanford University where she is working on a poetic rewrite of the US Department of Defense's dictionary. A 2011 winner of the Boston Review/"Discovery" Poetry Prize, her work has appeared in *jubilat*, *Kenyon Review*, *DIAGRAM*, *Gulf Coast*, and others.

Menka Shivdasani has authored two poetry collections, *Nirvana at Ten Rupees* and *Stet*, and is co-translator of Freedom and Fissures, an anthology of Sindhi Partition poetry. She has edited an anthology of women's writing for Sound and Picture Archives for Research on Women (SPARROW). Her career as a journalist includes the publication of eight books with Raju Kane, three of which were released by the then prime minister Atal Bihari Vajpayee. She played a key role in founding the Poetry Circle in Mumbai.

Evie Shockley is the author of two books of poetry, *a half-red sea* and *the new black*, which won the 2012 Hurston/Wright Legacy Award in poetry. She has also authored a critical study, *Renegade Poetics: Black Aesthetics and Formal Innovation in African American Poetry*, and serves as the creative writing editor for the journal Feminist Studies. Recipient of the 2012 Holmes National Poetry Prize, Shockley is Associate Professor of English at Rutgers University, New Brunswick.

Dinos Siotis was born in Tinos, Greece, in 1944. A poet, novelist and literary critic, he has published 20 books of poetry and fiction in English, French and Greek. In 2007 he received in Athens the State Prize for Poetry for his book *Autobiography of a Target*. He is the director of the Tinos International Literary Festival, president of Poets Circle in Greece, editor of *(de)kata* and *Poetix* and in charge of Global Communication for World Poetry Movement.

Ewa Sonnenberg (b. 1967) is the author of eight collections of poetry, including *Płonący tramwaj* [*Burning Tram*] and *Smycz* [*Leash*]. Her collection *Hazard* won the Georg Trakl Prize. Sonnenberg lives and works in Krakow.

Julia Stein's fifth book of poetry, *What Were They Like?*, was published in March 2013 and is about the Iraq War. She has previously published four books of poetry: from the feminist poetry work of her first book *Under the Ladder to Heaven* (1984), to her poetry about the Central American Wars in her second book *Desert Soldiers* (1992), to the love poems and poems about adjunct teaching in South Central Los Angeles during the 1992 troubles in *Walker Woman* (2004).

Paul Summers was born in the North East of England, in 1967. He now lives in Central Queensland. His poems have appeared widely in print since the late 1980s and he has performed all over the world. He has also written for TV, film, radio and theatre and has collaborated many times with other artists and musicians on mixed-media projects and public art. He won Northern Arts Writers Awards in 1995 and 1998 and a Northern Writers Award in 2008.

David Sullivan's first book, *Strong-Armed Angels*, was published by Hummingbird Press, and three of its poems were read by Garrison Keillor on The Writer's Almanac. *Every Seed of the Pomegranate*, a multi-voiced series of poems about the war in Iraq, was published by Telbot Bach. His book of co-translations of Adnan al-Sayegh's poetry just came out. He teaches at Cabrillo College, where he edits the Porter Gulch Review with his students, and lives in Santa Cruz, California

Lia Tarachansky is a Russian-Israeli journalist and filmmaker. She is the Israel/Palestine Correspondent for the independent global video agency The Real News Network, and her work has been featured in the *Huffington Post, USA Today*, and *Al Jazeera*. Her latest film, *Seven Deadly Myths*, looks at the biggest taboo in Israeli history—what happened in 1948—and how in recent years the government attempted to silence critical voices calling to revise the national narrative.

Tim Thorne, born in 1944, lives in Launceston, Australia. He is the author of 14 books of poetry and has been involved in peace and environmental campaigns all his adult life. In 2007 his *A Letter to Egon Kisch* won the William Baylebridge Award for the best Australian poetry book. Thorne was awarded the 2012 Christopher Brennan Award for a lifetime's achievement in Australian poetry.

Laura Tohe is Diné in Sleepy Rock clan born for the Bitter Water clan. A librettist and an award winning poet, her books include *No Parole Today* and *Code Talker Stories*. Her commissioned libretto, *Enemy Slayer, A Navajo Oratorio* made its world premiere in 2008 and was performed by The Phoenix Symphony Orchestra. She is Professor with Distinction in Indigenous Literature at Arizona State University.

Bill Tremblay is a poet, novelist, librettist, and reviewer. He founded the *Colorado Review* and served as chief editor for 15 years. His work has appeared in seven full-length volumes including his most recent book: *Magician's Hat: Poems on the Life and Art of David Alfaro Siqueiros* (Lynx House Press: 2013). He is author of a novel, *The June Rise* (Utah State University Press/Fulcrum Publishing) and the libretto for the operatic musical *Salem, 1692*. He received the John F. Stern Distinguished Professor Award in 2004.

Bunkong Tuon is a Cambodian-American writer, poet, and professor at Union College, in Schenectady, NY. His poetry and nonfiction have appeared in *The Massachusetts Review*, *The New York Quarterly*, *Numéro Cinq*, among other publications. *Gruel*, his first full-length collection of poems, will be published by NYQ Books in late 2014.

Brian Turner, born in 1967, is an American poet, essayist, and professor. He won the 2005 Beatrice Hawley Award for his debut collection, *Here, Bullet*, (Alice James Books) the first of many awards and honors received for this collection of poems about his experience as a soldier in the Iraq War. His honors since then include a Lannan Literary Fellowship and the prestigious Poet's

Prize (2007). His second collection, shortlisted for the 2010 T.S. Eliot Prize [2] is *Phantom Noise* (Alice James Books, 2010).

Douglas Valentine, the editor of this volume, is the author of four books of historical non-fiction: *The Hotel Tacloban; The Phoenix Program; The Strength of the Wolf: The Secret History of America's War on Drugs;* and *The Strength of the Pack: The Personalities, Politics and Espionage Intrigues that Shaped the DEA.* He is the author of one novel, *TDY,* and one book of poems, *A Crow's Dream.* He lives with his wife Alice in Massachusetts.

Dr. Vacy Vlazna is Coordinator of Justice for Palestine Matters. She was Human Rights Advisor to the GAM team in the second round of the Acheh peace talks, Helsinki, February 2005 then withdrew on principle. Vacy was coordinator of the East Timor Justice Lobby as well as serving in East Timor with UNAMET and UNTAET from 1999-2001. She came to Australia as a refugee from the Russian occupation of then Czechoslovakia.

Afaa Michael Weaver (Michael S. Weaver) is a veteran of 15 years as a factory worker in his native Baltimore. A poet, playwright, and translator, his twelfth and most recent collection of poetry is *The Government of Nature* (University of Pittsburgh Press, 2013). He has received two Pushcart prizes and a Fulbright appointment, among other honors. Afaa is Alumnae Professor of English at Simmons College and a visiting faculty member at Drew University's MFA program.

Bruce Weigl, born in 1949, is an American contemporary poet who teaches at Lorain County Community College. An American veteran of the Vietnam War, Weigl states in his memoir, *The Circle of Hanh* (2000), "The paradox of my life as a writer is that the war ruined my life and in return gave me my voice." Weigl's 13th collection of poems, *The Abundance of Nothing* (2012), was one of three finalists for the Pulitzer Prize. His poetry collection, *Song of Napalm* (1988), was also nominated for the Pulitzer Prize.

Makhosazana Xaba is currently a writing fellow at the Wits School of Public Health. She is the author of two poetry collections: *these hands* (2005) and *Tongues of their Mothers* (2008).

She is a co-editor, with Karen Martin, of *Queer Africa: New and Collected Fiction* (2013) and an author of *Running and Other Stories* (2013) her début collection of fiction. She is the winner of the 2005 Deon Hofmeyr Award for Creative Writing.

Phillippa Yaa de Villiers is a South African writer and performer whose collection *The Everyday Wife* won the 2011 SALA award for poetry. Her work has been translated into Italian, German and Mandarin, and appears in local and international journals and anthologies. Her play *Original Skin* tours locally and internationally.

Müesser Yeniay was born in İzmir, in 1984. She is currently pursuing a PhD in Turkish literature. A recipient of several poetry prizes in Turkey, her verse has been translated into several languages. She is the editor of the literature magazine Şiirden. Her books are: *Dibine Düşüyor Karanlık da* (2009), *Evimi Dağlara Kurdum* (2010), *Yeniden Çizdim Göğü* (2011),and Öteki *Bilinç* (2013). She has translated Behruz Kia, Michel Cassir, Gerard Augustin and the Contemporary Spanish Poetry Anthology into Turkish.

Daisy Zamora is one of the most prominent figures in contemporary Latin American poetry. Her work is known for its uncompromising voice and wide-ranging subject matter that dwells on the details of daily life while encompassing human rights, politics, revolution, feminist issues, art, history and culture. She has received several literary awards. Her poetry, essays and articles have been published throughout Latin America, the Caribbean, Canada, the U.S., Europe, Asia and Australia.